Me, My Morgan & Th

Me, My Morgan & The Midlands

Michael Pearson

WAYZGOOSE

Published by Wayzgoose 2002

Michael Pearson asserts the moral right to be
identified as the author of this work.

Wayzgoose
Tatenhill Common
Staffordshire
DE13 9RS
Tel: 01283 713674
enquiries@wayzgoose.org.uk

ISBN 0 907864 95 3

A CIP catalogue entry for this book is available from
the British Library.

Printed by STIGE, Via Pescarito 110, 10099 San
Mauro, Torino, Italy.

*Special thanks to Mark Ledington, Charles Morgan,
Cristina Negri, Jackie Pearson and Karen Tanguy.*

Contents

It is safe to say that, having known Michael Pearson for as long as I can remember, I never expected that he would ever take to the road in a bright yellow sports car. Bus, barge, bicycle and branchline train are the modes of transport one associates with this most lyrical of topographical writers. The surprise acquisition of a Morgan Plus 8 for this latest literary adventure is as astonishing and improbable as the Pope turning up for Easter Mass in Rome with Sophia Loren draped laconically over his arm.

Personally, I suspect market forces are at work. Is this a last ditch attempt to court the kind of popularity he had hitherto been happy to ignore? His devotees, among whom I am proud to number myself, must hope that his unlikely embrace of roads and motor cars does not prove permanent and exclusive. The canal and railway books he has been churning out for the best part of a quarter of a century rarely rose beyond the confines of their cult status, but their integrity was transparent.

Nevertheless, I commend *Me, My Morgan & The Midlands* to all who have treasured and enjoyed Michael Pearson's previous output. Once I had got over the shock of seeing him metaphorically disappearing down the road in a cloud of dust, I relished every word and every photograph of this lively new book. Profundity, insight, humour, and that trademark knack of making us all think we are part of the experience - all the usual ingredients are included. But an additional theme emerges now that the author has reached what Arnold Bennett once called the interesting, tender and romantic age of fifty. Hitherto disarmingly boyish - long after the abrasive absurdities of adult life should have beaten it out of him, I sense a sudden realisation in this new book that the second half is underway and that there are tackles to be made and goals to be scored before the final, irrevocable whistle blows. The spur is not fame, he once confided, tongue loosened by Woodforde's Wherry bitter in a low-beamed, flagstoned public bar on the North Norfolk coast, just a modest, unostentatious quota of immortality.

Miles Platting

Map reading on the top of the Herefordshire Beacon, Malvern Hills

Ledbury to HEREFORDSHIRE Lucton

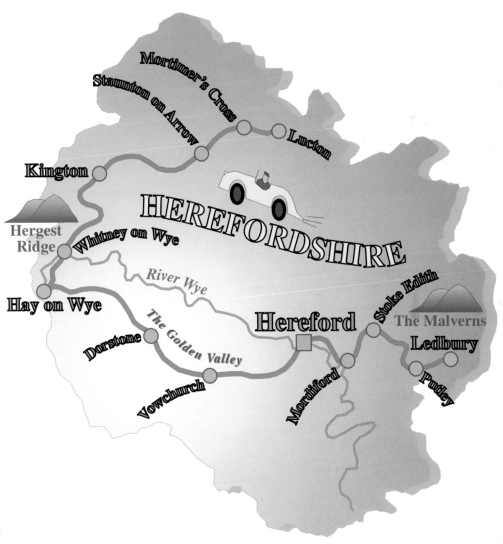

"Darling," called Jackie over the rim of *The Independent* one damp and desultory April afternoon. "What would you like for your fiftieth, a new car or one of those surprise birthday parties where all your friends and relatives hide in a darkened room, until you come in, and then they switch the lights on and shriek 'Happy Birthday'?"

"Hmm, I'm not sure," I replied tentatively, because if the truth were known I hadn't really been listening, and I thought the best thing to do was to play for time, and see if she would give herself away.

"Of course a car would be more expensive, but when you think about it, all the drink and all the food, not to mention all the damage that your wild friends inevitably wreak, would soon add up to probably just as much."

"I expect you're right," I agreed, though still somewhat in the dark as to the gist of the conversation.

"And you don't like many people anyway, and most of your relations are either dead or in exile, so I think we should go for the car. One of those nice new Minis, perhaps. Then we could all drive it."

"Whatever you say, darling," I said brightly, already back on the sports page ...

The upshot of that soliloquy was that, on my fiftieth birthday I went down to Malvern to collect a Morgan. Yes a *hand-built* Morgan sports car, not a *mass-produced* Mini. Apparently Jackie hadn't been able to find Mini in the directory - very likely, I quipped, when she told me, because they are German-owned nowadays. Not to be denied, she'd sensibly gone for the next car manufacturer alphabetically, not perhaps realising that a Morgan might cost slightly more than a Mini. "But it's not everyday that you're fifty, darling," she reassured me soothingly when the bill finally plopped through the letter box with a distinctive thud. "And you can always write a book and put it on expenses," she added.

I wasn't feeling old, let alone middle-aged, I just felt as I had always done - age*less*. Sometimes, between you and me, I *do* worry that my brain has not kept pace with the ageing process: my brain thinks it's still twenty-something, my body knows better; my brain assumes the world is still its oyster, my body worries that it won't be up to the long walk home after the last metaphorical bus has gone. I can still beat my eleven year old son for pace on the football field, but only when I surreptitiously tie his shin pads together beforehand. All the things that captured my imagination at ten, twenty, thirty and forty - from sausage & chips to Rachmaninov's piano concertos - I still embrace enthusiastically.

Of course there are a few refinements: the acquired nuances of wisdom, a clearer grasp of the rise and fall of Lancashire's textile industry, a cynically acquired appreciation of the rampant greed of building societies; and a few casualties, passing proprietary fads: Blue Nun, Tamla Motown and Old Spice. I needed a new car to take my mind off the march of time. The last time I'd had a new car to mark a birthday was a Vauxhall Victor in 1961, with Dinky embossed on the bottom. But a Morgan, now we're talking; the stuff of motoring legend, the stuff of male fantasy, the sort of car that old associates would see me flashing by in, and realise that they'd always underestimated that chap Pearson.

When, in 1990, the television troubleshooter, Sir John Harvey-Jones visited the Morgan works to make a programme for the BBC, he asked the foreman of the chassis shop how long he had worked for the company and was told 'thirty years'.

"You must have seen a lot of changes," remarked Sir John.

"No, not really," came the reply.

That was the cue for Sir John to launch into diatribes of business-school invective concerning mechanisation and productivity - double price, triple output, you know the sort of thing - but it missed the point. Morgan have stayed in business for almost a hundred years precisely because they haven't kept pace with progress, they've gone off on a different journey altogether, and a much more enjoyable one at that. Tradition is the most important element in their continued success - people don't buy Morgan sports cars because they are of antique appearance, but because they are *timeless*, which is a much more difficult feat to achieve.

Remarkably, the Morgan Motor Company is a three generation family concern. Its founder, Henry Frederick Stanley Morgan was born in Moreton Jeffries, Herefordshire in 1881, the son of the rector of Stoke Lacy. He was despatched to prep school in Broadstairs where he was mechanically enough minded to invent a three-nib pen to speed up the writing of punishment lines. Marlborough followed, but proved an unhappy experience and his family took him out, content to let him complete his secondary education with a series of trips to Europe in the manner of the Grand Tour. He became a keen amateur photographer, but mechanical matters were his first love and he furthered his education at the Crystal Palace College of Engineering. An apprenticeship with the Great Western Railway in Swindon followed where he worked with William Dean and George Jackson Churchward - the railways were ironically a fertile breeding ground for motor engineers - but all the time H. F. S. Morgan was growing more and more interested in the burgeoning world of motoring. He left the Great Western in 1905 (the same year that Herbert Austin opened his car factory at Longbridge, twenty miles to the north) and set up in business as a garage owner in Malvern Link offering 'all kinds of repairs executed by competent workmen and first-class machinery'. Slowly, though hardly dramatically, the business began to pay its way, and for a while it also operated bus services in the Malvern district. By 1909, however, H. F. S. was busy developing a tiller-steered three wheeler with the help of the engineering master of Malvern College. Powered by a 7hp Peugeot engine, its first outing was to Shelsley Walsh in hilly Herefordshire. A two seater version was exhibited at Olympia two years later, and if you had then and there placed an order for the top of the range model it would have set you back £96!

I wasn't convinced that I had come to the right place. The building looked as if it might contain a small foundry or be the premises of a greetings card manufacturer. But in reception I was reassured by a plethora of Morgan memorabilia, and by the fact that they seemed to be expecting me. Not that being 'expected' is always a wholly reliable sign. When I was eighteen I was interviewed for the post of headmaster at a Derby primary school because it was next door to the Art School where they were patiently awaiting my arrival for a foundation-course appraisal session. Personally I blame the school secretary. She asked me if I'd come about the interview, and I simply said "yes". Needless to add, I didn't get the job. Which was rather a shame because I hated every minute of art school, largely because my enrolment coincided with an era where the last thing they wanted to teach you at art school was how to paint.

A young man called Mark Ledington had been delegated to show me over the car - you see how it is being fifty, suddenly not only policemen but also the employees of hand-built sports car companies seem much younger than you are. I thought it not worth mentioning to Mark that I had never been in a sports car before - I've led a very sheltered life, none of my girl friends owned one. My car was in the body shop, looking rather splendid and racy in its sober yellow livery. I made an immediate mental note to keep rigidly to the speed limit in future, this was not a car to ever go unnoticed in. Mark ran through things in a perfunctory manner, we were, after all, men of the motoring world, fellow aficionados tacitly familiar with what went on under the bonnet.

It became apparent that I was expected to reverse out of the workshop. These days Morgan employ around a hundred and fifty people, and I had the distinct impression that they had all come to watch me. Getting into the Morgan was like getting into bed, I looked up in case Mark was going to hand me a mug of Horlicks, but he was just smiling, waiting for me to turn the windscreen wipers off.

"Bear in mind that it doesn't have power steering," called Mark as I tentatively began to move backwards in the general, though not specific, direction of the doors.

"Ha, ha," I laughed, as if power steering and similarly sybaritic accessories were anathema to an enthusiast such as I. Suddenly I was aware of a commotion behind me and glancing round saw several men manhandling oil drums out of my path. I waved nonchalantly, as if magnanimously acknowledging their error in leaving the drums there in the first place. I suppose there was room to fit a fine tooth comb between the car's gleaming bodywork and the edge of the

doorway, but only just. It was a relief to be out in the open air. Mark certainly had a point about the power steering, I've operated sluice gates which demanded less effort. I turned left out of the factory gate, not because I wanted to go that way, but because it seemed the easier option ...

*   *   *

Prior to battle, know your ground. Sound military tactics had led me to the crown of the Herefordshire Beacon and the whole county lay, beguilingly full of poetry, possibility and potential, at my feet, a chiaroscuro of light and shade under cumulus-clouded skies. The dashing yellow Morgan was sunning itself in the car park at Wynds Point while its driver puffed and panted his way to the Beacon's 1,114ft summit, walking under larksong in the footsteps of Caractacus, the ancient Briton who had fought and lost against the Romans on these steep slopes in 55AD. I doubted if it had been a fair fight, how could anyone have concentrated on blood and thunder in the face of such beauty? I would have been easy meat for any Centurion, my gaze held on the heavenly view westwards towards Wales, a dreaming fool, slain by inattentiveness as once I would be tackled with the ball while watching out for passing trains beyond the school playing fields.

But the Malverns are made for dreamers, and they were out in numbers on this bright June morning, walking their dogs or just walking themselves, until reaching the rounded ramparts at the top, where they'd stand with 'foolish grins keeping perfectly still' like the Lennon & McCartney song from *A Magical Mystery Tour*. I sat on the grass and attempted to lay my map out in front of me, so as to plan my own mystery tour, but a playful little breeze had other ideas, turning the map into a kite and almost ripping it from my grasp. I could see for miles: to the Black Mountains and Radnor Forest, and it seemed to me lying there - fifty something and feeling it - that the journeys one elects to make are every bit as significant as friendships; relationships to be savoured and chosen carefully,

Sheltering from the showers - Ledbury Market House

Walking away from the station - Ledbury

the chaff shaken out and disposed of.

In the middle distance stood Eastnor Castle and its prominent parkland obelisk, a memorial to members of the family who fell on foreign fields. Eastnor makes me think of two things: the televised version of John Masefield's *Box of Delights*, parts of which were filmed there; and a walk I did on a foggy day for a book called *Cotswolds & Malverns Railway Rides*, a day made memorable by a close encounter with a stag. Beyond Eastnor the rooftops of Ledbury were discernible, though currently in shadow, and further to the right, Oyster Hill, where Elizabeth Barrett Browning spent her childhood. So much for topography and literary association, it was time to be off. Going downhill - not so taxing on one's stamina, but more painful on one's legs - I encountered a simple bench engraved with the names 'Ted & Peggy Hill'. How nice to have your

existence and your marriage remembered in such a way. I think I would rather be commemorated thus than by any amount of spurious fame or accolade.

Quarter past ten was striking as I drove into Ledbury, and the friendly cotton wool clouds had turned ominously black. Jackie and I first knew the town in the Seventies when it was our habit to camp in a thistley field at the back of a pub in nearby Ashperton, so as to be able to attend the Malvern Festival of an evening. We heard a cherubic Nigel Kennedy play the Mendelssohn concerto, and a perspiring Pinchas Zukerman play the Elgar; but even more remarkable was the occasion we stood next to Michael Tippet while he judged the festival's marmalade making competition. It was like standing in the same room as an archangel, and I swear we could feel the flapping of his wings.

More recently, we lunched rather well at The Feathers on the way back from a first meeting with our new black Labrador, Ely, born and bred at Hellens, Much Marcle. So Ledbury is a town with happy memories for me, and I enjoyed revisiting it, dodging the showers by sheltering under the half-timbered Market House and briefly embracing an indoor bric-a-brac fair from which I miraculously escaped without emptying the contents of my wallet.

In the Tourist Information Centre I asked about hops. Hopyards have always interested me since I first saw them, stretching in highly strung rows beside the lovely railway line which runs from Worcester to Hereford. Subsequent literary encounters with hop growing in novels by Francis Brett Young, John Moore and Sheila Kaye Smith nourished my enthusiasm. Was there, I asked the helpful ladies behind the counter, a nearby hopyard open to the public? I was enthusiastically pointed in the direction of Bromyard Heritage Centre which hosts an exhibition entitled 'The Year of the Hop', which would have been ideal had Bromyard been on or remotely near my itinerary. Sadly it wasn't, and this being my first journey, I was loath to abandon my plans too early in the proceedings, for fear that anarchy would set in. I didn't discourage the ladies with such details, and left with cheerful injunctions to enjoy my day. Neither did I explain the purpose of my enquiries, ever since I started writing guide books a natural reticence usually pulls me up short of exposing the motives behind my questioning. Sometimes this approach may cost me dear, mostly I think it spares me from a good deal of useless information and misplaced parochial pride.

I was a week or two too early for Ledbury's Poetry Festival, which the Poet Laureate had recently proclaimed 'the best in the country'. I am sure that this had nothing to do with the fact that he was launching the festival. The programme made mouth-watering reading. I would have liked to have been in Ledbury to attend a lecture on Robert Frost at Hellens, or to go on the John Masefield Walk. Frost was one of the so called 'Dymock Poets' who, in 1914, congregated at the Gloucestershire village of that name, located some four miles south of Ledbury. His sojourn lasted barely a year, during which local gossip had it that he was a German spy, but it was a fertile period for this most definitive of country poets, and he was joined for a time by another of my heroes, Edward Thomas.

Ledbury was Masefield's boyhood home, and that wonderful children's

The Post Office at Putley

book *The Box of Delights* is set loosely in the area. Besides, had life taken a different turn, I might have been declaiming my own poetry to eager festival-goers. After all, my poem *Sunday in the Garden* came second in the York Schools Poetry Competition of 1968, and would have perhaps won if I hadn't chosen to wear a tweed hat adorned with fisherman's flies to the judging ceremony in the - what I can now see as mistaken - belief that it afforded me a Bohemian air of mystery.

A by-road led me out of Ledbury to Little Marcle, where I crossed the A417 (which had once been a Roman Road) and made for Putley, largely because lots of orchards were marked on the Ordnance Survey map and I thought there might be hopyards also. In this I was wrong, but by way of consolation I was introduced to an attractive little village still retaining a brick-built post office.

"Nice to see a post office still open in a village as small as this," I remarked to the lady behind the counter.

"Ah, but they keep trying to shut us down," she retorted.

"Who do?"

"This Consignia lot," she laughed bitterly, as if any organisation crazy

In the hopyards of Herefordshire - Stoke Edith

enough to re-brand themselves with such a name was very likely incapable of making commercially astute decisions in any case.

I came upon two racehorses being exercised on the edge of the village, pulled up to let them pass, and got thanked for my trouble by a strong Irish accent explaining that his mount was: "a young horse, never been out before." I trust it would be explained to him that not all motor cars he would encounter would be so garishly coloured nor so noisy.

Remembering that there were hopyards between the railway and the A438, I left Putley in a northerly direction and proceeded to Stoke Edith. I was conscious that I was getting nowhere fast, but it didn't seem to matter. I had no appointments to keep. Each day would be tailored to my own whims, or, even better, to fate. I had deliberately decided to avoid pre-arrranged meetings with the sort of 'interesting' personalities featured in other books. What conversations I would have, would be 'chance encounters' for real. I had one of these just outside Stoke Edith. There was a large field of hops growing alongside the main road, and from a man in a nearby farmyard I learned that they were very probably of the Wye Target variety and that after they had grown to the top of their poles, and been harvested in the autumn, they'd be bought by a brewery, though which he wouldn't like to say. As a beer drinker, I looked upon the fledgling hops as a gamekeeper might regard his pheasant chicks, in mouth-watering anticipation of the feast ahead.

Leaving the main road at Dormington I drove through the valley of the River Frome to Mordiford where an ancient bridge spans the Lugg, just short of its confluence with the Wye. The bridge has nine arches and dates from the 14th and 16th centuries. In normal conditions only two arches span the river, but at times of flood it widens its shoulders and waters them all. A mansion called Sufton overlooks the scene, whilst to the east wooded hills provide a picturesque backdrop to a village which has legendary connections with a dragon who devoured a lot of locals before being slain by a man disguised as a barrel of cider, the moral of which is that you should never trust a barrel that you haven't been formally introduced to.

On the way into Hereford I passed a pub called the Bunch of Carrotts and the premises of the Wye Valley Brewery, purveyors of Dorothy Goodbody's seasonal ales. I began to grow thirsty. Travelling as lightly as was practical, the bulk of my luggage on these county explorations amounted to a copy of the appropriate *Shell Guide*, ditto One Inch Ordnance Survey map, and the CAMRA *Good Beer Guide*, deeming all other items unessential.

The bridge across the Lugg at Mordiford

I was familiar with at least one visual aspect of Hereford long before I really got to know the city, for, in 1972, I had painted a view of the Wye Bridge and the Cathedral purloined from a photograph in a 1950s British Railways Holiday Guide. The painting now hangs in my parents' home, the cynosure of every visitor's eye. Many an embarrassing conversational pause has been saved by its admiration, though one of their more intellectually-minded acquaintances took satisfaction in pointing out that it wasn't, in his opinion, an *original* Constable.

Again, it was in the (in retrospect) halcyon days of the Seventies that we grew familiar with Hereford in the flesh, changing here from train to bus on sorties out to the secondhand bookshops of Hay-on-Wye. Once we had time for a fleeting visit to the Cathedral to see the Mappa Mundi, and now I was making a sentimental journey to see it again, freshly interested in it from a cartographer's viewpoint, after twenty years of professional (in the sense that I get paid for it) map-making of my own.

Sun now warm on my back, I strode instinctively out in the direction of the Cathedral, never having ventured into Hereford in a motor car before, and knowing only my whereabouts in relation to the railway station and the cattle market. Sure enough, I found it looming at the end of Castle Street. Stonemasons were working openly and diligently on the restoration of the

The Wye at Hereford

Lady Chapel. Their activity seemed anachronistic. At breaktimes I imagined scenes of horseplay and bawdy badinage in an unintelligible 13th century dialect; faces being pulled at passing wenches like the gargoyles whose impish grins they were so painstakingly replicating.

One doesn't pay to go into the Cathedral - though donations are tacitly encouraged - but one does part with cash to see the Chained Library and the World Map. The display I had paid to see was succinctly informative. Amongst other things, I learned that the Mappa Mundi originated, not in Hereford, as one might leap to assume, but in Lincoln. It dates possibly from 1280 and was the work of one Richard de Bello who bequeathed it to Hereford in 1330. It lives (and I use that verb deliberately) in a cool, dark dungeon like room, which I presume is a measure taken to increase its lifespan. It reminded me of nothing so much as a diagram of the human alimentary canal, but I was in hushed awe of its beauty and resilience, and I could have gazed raptly at it for hours had half of Herefordshire not lain in wait for me. The uncanny thing about its depiction of the British Isles was how like an embryo it looked, a womb like approximation of the shape so scientifically calibrated that we know today. The Chained Library is of the 12th Century. The interpretive panel put it rather neatly: 'In the Middle Ages books were rare and so was honesty' (no change there, then) 'so they were kept under lock and key'. Back in the Cathedral itself, the nave was beginning to fill for an organ recital by Geraint Bowen. I would very much have liked to loiter and listen, Choral Evensong at 5.30pm was also tempting, but the very nature of these whistlestop tours I had undertaken demanded stern sacrifices to perpetual motion.

I grabbed a smoked salmon baguette from a lively sandwich bar in Church Street and made for the hills, pulling a flanker on the Golden Valley by way of Clehonger and Kingstone. Something must have gone awry in the memory bank, for I remembered a much prettier approach than this, a winding road punctuated by handsome stone villages of steeply clustered buildings. The B4349 I found myself on was a bit bland. I

put the discrepancy down to memory loss, already apparently taking its toll. At this rate I might never find my way home.

The concept behind each motor tour was that I should stay within the confines of the nominated county, but already I was weakening. The bookshops of Hay-on-Wye beguiled me. I had made up a bit of time with my quick getaway from Hereford, and there had been no dawdling in the Golden Valley, so three quarters of an hour in Hay would do me no harm, I reasoned with my conscience, a likeably malleable cove, not unresponsive to a jolly jape here or a merry wheeze there. Arm in arm we conspiratorially slipped over the border at Cusop, abandoned the Morgan to the bovine gaze of Hay's natives, and began our bibliophilic interlude in the world famous Hay Cinema Bookshop.

Nowadays Hay seems a lot more savvy, more worldly-wise, than when Jackie and I first made pilgrimages here to worship at the shrine of the self-styled King of Hay, Richard Booth. The in joke then was that Hay was a principality in its own right, and that Booth held sway over a growing kingdom whose sole industry was the regeneration of secondhand books. We came by bus because it was more romantic to do so, and because Jackie was more happy to indulge my idiosyncrasies then. Between bookshops we would wander down to the high bridge over the river and watch huge salmon basking in the Wye. In those days we collected James Hilton and Sheila Kaye Smith, J. B. Priestley and Daphne Du Maurier. The novelists one has phases for define the epochs of one's life. In childhood I devoured Anthony Buckeridge and Richmal Crompton, at school Buchan and Household, at college D. H. Lawrence, T. H. White and Herman Hesse. Now my literary heroes are William Trevor and J. L. Carr, and I find it hard to believe that anyone will ever replace them.

Nothing particular caught my eye in the Cinema, so I walked along to Richard Booth's Bookshop on Lion Street which is habitually said to stock something not far short of a half a million titles. Like Mark Twain, I saw through numbers a long time ago. Booth's stock - at least the topography section which I paid most attention to - seemed tired and tawdry. Too many of the books on sale were ex public library cast offs: not second-hand books so much as hundred and thousand-hand; grubby and tainted with nicotine. If you were desperate for the information or entertainment they contained, all well and good, but they were too far gone to give a good home to. Untempted and dispirited, I crossed the alley to Cooke & Sons and encountered similarly lacklustre stock all over again. It was as if the monster of book town was being fed on a cheap diet of the literary equivalent of pig swill. It was as if tourists, who knew no better, were being fobbed off with books by the yard. The funny thing about second hand books is that they multiply exponentially all the time. As children we think comfortingly of heaven being filled with the happy souls of everyone who has ever lived. Adulthood renders this logistically implausible. Likewise the world is slowly but surely growing heavier and heavier with books. There is not room for them all, so they end up in Hay-on-Wye and all its weary, worldwide imitators.

Booth's Bookshop, Hay-on-Wye

The 'King's' castle - Hay-on-Wye

Thus I drove out of Hay, uniquely, without adding to my library, whose groaning shelves would be grateful. I only had to go a few hundred yards to be back in England, and I followed the Wye upstream through the village of Clifford. It felt good to be back in the fresh air. My anger with Hay subsided. It had been a little spat, nothing more. Next time I would fall upon a treasure and all would be forgiven. Whitney Toll Bridge revived my spirits. Ancient and incongruous, I was happy to part with money to pass over it. Few motorists would subscribe to my theory that road-pricing would be a good thing. In a perfect world all travel would cost nothing but the participant's time, public and private transport alike paid out of taxes. But until the politicians engineer such a Shangri-La, it seems to me unfair that road transport should effectively be 'free'.

A short sprint along the A438 was enough for me. The traffic resented my stately progress. I was beginning to appreciate that sports cars are viewed as a challenge to a certain kind of motorist, I believe Irish Wolfhounds have the same effect on Jack Russells. I turned left into Whitney-on-Wye and left again at Millhalf, heading back towards the Welsh border at Brilley Mountain. Through deep lanes of foxgloves I drove, swerving once to avoid collision with a small red bus which came round a corner like a rampaging Hereford bull. In front of me lay the bare sweep of Hergest Ridge which gave its name to Mike Oldfield's rather less successful follow up to *Tubular Bells*. But it was the music of a far less well known composer which had drawn me to this remote corner of Herefordshire. Ernest John ('my friends call me Jack') Moeran lived on and off in Kington during the 1940s. Born in 1884, of Anglo-Irish parentage, he spent most of his childhood in Norfolk, where his Irish father was a clergyman. Educated at Uppingham and the Royal College of Music, during the First World War a piece of shrapnel unobligingly embedded itself so close to his brain that doctors would not attempt to remove it. This souvenir was to have repercussions on his life thereafter, not least a propensity for drinking binges, which those favourably disposed towards him believed were driven by the need from time to time to deflect the pain.

Moeran's dual parentage left him with a foot in both camps, and his orchestral music, songs and chamber works are imbued with the landscapes of England and Ireland. Spiritually he felt more akin with the latter. Perhaps this persuaded him into an ill-conceived marriage in 1945 to the feisty Irish cellist, Peers Coetmore, an effectively short-lived union whose offspring was not a child but a cello concerto of astonishing beauty. Jack Moeran spent more and more time in Kenmare, County Kerry, while Peers Coetmore toured the world. In 1950 he fell from the pier at Kenmare and drowned. Some rumours suggested he was drunk, others that it was an act of suicide by a depressed man. More kindly, a cerebral haemorrhage was hinted at.

Moeran's connections with Kington were as a result of his parents retiring there. The Herefordshire and Radnor scenery is said to have inspired a number of his works, most notably the *Sinfonietta*, a lively and charming piece which reminds you of Elgar's *Introduction and Allegro* at first, before firmly evoking its own alternately plaintive and rumbustious soundworld. I stumbled upon it on a disc of Holst and Bax around 1970, but it was the discovery of a recording of his *Cello Concerto* in Gibb's Bookshop, Manchester which certified me as a Moeran fan. Recorded by Lyrita, who championed many neglected British composers back in those vinyl days, the cover featured a gorgeous sepia photograph of Jack Moeran and Peers Coetmore by the toposcope at the top of the Worcester Beacon on the Malvern Hills. The original had been taken by

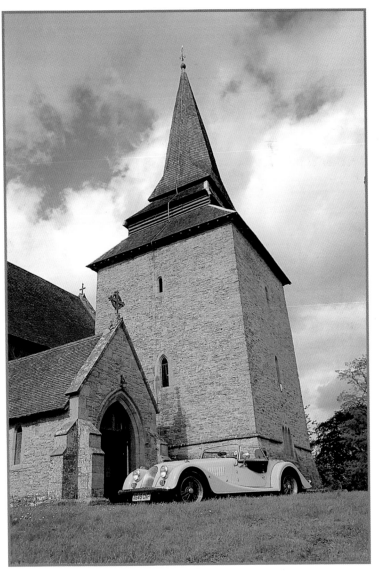

St Mary's, Kington

Gravel Hill, E.J. Moeran's parent's house in Kington

Dick Jobson, a then young Kington doctor and keen amateur photographer who had become firm friends with Jack, not least because of their shared enthusiasm for railways. Years later I came upon the doctor's photography again in a book by Nicholas de Courtais about the Radnor railway. I treasure these small coincidences, these random jigsaw pieces in a greater puzzle. Dick Jobson remained a country doctor in Kington until his death in 1977. Twenty-five years later I was driving into town in my Morgan on the lookout for momentoes of Moeran.

I didn't know whether to be happy or sad that Kington seemed oblivious to E. J. Moeran. Of course to a certain extent we like to clasp our heroes to our bosom, resentful when the greater world wants a share of them. I never quite got over the virtually unknown Bruce Springsteen of *The Wild, the Innocent & the East Street Shuffle* becoming the world famous megastar of *Born in the USA*. Jack Moeran is in no danger of such fame. Though he has a loyal web site of followers, the inhabitants of Kington seem impervious to

his memory. Neither the Tourist Information Centre nor the Kington Museum made mention of him. The former was more concerned with passing backpackers on the Offa's Dyke long distance path, the latter with the strange story of a circus elephant which died in the town in 1932. According to contemporary newspaper accounts 'the animal was walking from Leominster to Kington when it became ill. On arrival Mr W. Munslow, veterinary surgeon, was called but despite best attention the animal, said to be forty-seven years of age and weighing two and a half tons, died.' There is an even sadder postscript, for in 1988 the elephant's remains were accidentally disinterred by a JCB.

There was no charge to visit the little museum, but a donation was discreetly solicited. I plopped a couple of pounds in the collection box. The elephant story alone was worth every penny. It belonged to Chapman's Gigantic Zoo-Circus which, if the advertisements were to be believed, was on its first tour out of London. Tigers, lions, polar bears, black comedy bears, elephants and boxing kangaroos were promised, all adding up to twenty-eight of the finest circus acts ever seen in England. Boomerang, the boxing kangaroo, would fight a few rounds with H. Wroe, the Australian boxer. Captain Kovah's eight 'awe-inspiring' tigers would be put through their paces. Mr Wagenaar and Miss Fossett would perform daring routines on the flying trapeze, as would the Whirlwind Wonder in her famous Voltage Act. Kington must have found it hard to contain its excitement.

E. J. Moeran married Peers Coetmore at St Mary's church. Wedding photographs depict a vivacious bride in a short skirted suit and a solemn groom who looks nonplussed by the proceedings. Inside the church seems deceptively spacious - that is to say its interior appears larger than the outside dimensions would appear to permit. I signed the visitors book, teasingly adding that I was in search of 'EJM'. From the church I traced Jack's uncertain footsteps down to the Old Tavern, his favoured watering hole. Frustratingly it wasn't open for business, otherwise I would have downed a pint in his memory. Gravel Hill, the Georgian house his parents lived in stood screened from the main road, a few hundred yards away. I summoned up the nerve to walk up its driveway, and rang the doorbell to ask permission to take a photograph of it. There was no reply, but as I turned to leave a man appeared from around the corner of the house and not unpleasantly asked if he could help me.

"I expect you can guess why I'm here," I said.

"Oh yes, we get a few of you," he responded, "more since the web site was started up. But by all means take a photograph." And with that, he strode off down the drive and out through the gate, as if to leave a perfect stranger taking photographs of your house because it once belonged to the parents of a little-known classical music composer was the most natural thing in the world. Jack Moeran would have warmed to that. Sixty years ago he might have warmed to me. We could have gone down to the Tavern for a pint or three, before hitching a lift on the pick-up goods to New Radnor, savouring the rhythm of a Great Western tank locomotive shuffling up the lush valley. Time passes down tunes and we hum them as if they were our own. Gerald Finzi, a rather less neglected composer, put it rather well: "I like to think in each generation may be found a few responsive minds. To shake hands with a good friend over the centuries is a pleasant thing."

I headed east out of Kington on the A44, but only as far as Lyonshall, beyond which I took to a wide but lonely by-road which led me over the River Arrow to Byton Hand. At Stockley Cross I came upon a charming cast iron finger post directing travellers to Staunton-on-Arrow, Titley and Lyonshall. Kington was given the option of two directions, but Pembridge and Shobdon must have lost their original sign, for a bland modern replacement had been added, spoiling the original's handsome ironwork. We seem to have lost the art of signwriting. Modern traffic appears to demand big, brash signposts, which, especially in rural environments, are totally out of keeping with the scale and character of their setting. The resultant eyesores often disfigure their locale. We need a new government department of unimpeachable aesthetic integrity to rid the world of such ugliness.

Thought it was not a Thursday, and barely any longer an afternoon, David Delaney, the amiable present owner of Mortimers Cross Mill very kindly opened its doors just for me. Driving a bright yellow Morgan sports car, I was beginning to appreciate, was like having a beautiful woman on your arm, doors firmly shut swing open with surprising ease. The gateway leading down to the mill and its bosky setting on the River Lugg was extremely narrow. In reverse it took a good deal of negotiating. There was a battle at Mortimers Cross during the Wars of the Roses. It took place on St Blaises Day in February 1461 and a lot of the casualties owed their death to the freezing waters of the river rather than the opposition's aggression. Mr Delaney issues visitors with a detailed account of the day's fighting and

Moeran's drinking hole - the Old Tavern, Kington

one room of the mill is given over to an exhibition of the battle. But this period of history is something of a mystery to me. The expensive boarding school I went to considered history and geography inappropriate bedfellows at O Level. And even when, reluctantly abandoning the study of history, for what I considered the slightly more interesting subject of geography, I was short-changed, being tutored in the formation of glacial moraines and the exports of Venezuela when all I really wanted to do was learn more and more and more about the coloured counties of England, Scotland and Wales. Things came to a head when I argued angrily in front of the whole class with one geography master over whether Mold was in Cheshire or the County of Flint. He favoured the former and carried the day on account of his superior standing. But I knew I was correct in believing the latter, and I don't think master or pupil had much time for each other from that day

wheel comes along a leat from a weir on the Lugg, and when it springs into life it can produce twelve horse power. There are three sets of grindstones, two of Derbyshire gritstone, the other, rather romantically, from Rouen in France. One of David Delaney's many visitors has been a lady called Florrie Dukes who lived here in 1919. Ostensibly she was employed as a housemaid but escaped to help the miller whenever the opportunity arose. A little booklet is on sale outlining her memories of life in and around the mill. She was fourteen years old and seven stones when she first came to Mortimers Cross to work. Two months later she weighed nine and a half stones: 'That was a good bit of grub I had, all bacon, boiled ham and home-made bread.' In winter, she and the miller found their way around the mill by candlelight. When she came back she and David discovered a half burned candle of hers in a dusty corner of the mill.

Being the owner and operator of a watermill, I have often thought, would come close to an ideal occupation, especially if I could operate a small clinker built ferry boat on the side. David, however, held no illusions. "It was hard and dangerous work," he told me as he locked up the mill until the next Thursday afternoon and saw me out of the narrow driveway, denting, but not destroying, my idyllic misconceptions.

I drove east along the B4362 towards the county boundary at Wooferton. The next village I came to was called Lucton, and knowing his habit of using place names for those of his characters, it occurred to me that Francis Brett Young had very probably derived the name of the eponymous hero of *Mr Lucton's Freedom* from here. This 1940 novel is a picaresque account of Owen Lucton, a successful and respected banker aged fifty from Birmingham, who briefly escapes from the responsibility of work and the indifference of his family, crashes his Pearce-Tregaron into a stream near Pershore and embarks upon a series of adventures involving haymaking, an excessively garrulous hiker who snores, the inevitable damsel in distress, a cricket match, a period as an odd job man, and eventual reconciliation with the real world. Thus Lucton seemed a significant and appropriate place to be ending my first adventure. Owen Lucton and I had age and outlook and an apptitude for adventure in common. I just prayed that my fast car wouldn't end up in the bed of a stream on any of the journeys to come.

forward. Education is like a sawmill - you deliver young trees and watch it turn them into planks.

Mortimers Cross Mill was first recorded in existence about the time of the battle, it probably dates back even further. Its working life continued until late in the 1940s. In its final years it was worked by a young woman in her early twenties because her father, the miller, had crushed his arm in the machinery. Restored by the Ministry of Works and under a deed of guardianship with English Heritage, it is open to the general public on Thursday afternoons from April to September between the hours of two and five-thirty. Occasionally its ancient machinery clatters into life to grind fodder for the rare breeds on the mill farm. But, of course, on the afternoon of my unexpected visit all was still, even if the mill was palpably 'breathing', like a sleeping old countryman of ancient years. The machinery in the mill now dates from 1871. The water to drive its middle breast shot

The Mill at Mortimers Cross

'From Clee to heaven' - the by-road to Cleobury

Shifnal to SHROPSHIRE Shrewsbury

Favourites are the prerogative of bookmakers, schoolmistresses and prime ministers picking cabinets. Travel writers risk censure and rebuke if they show evidence of bias, so please don't tell anyone that Shropshire, Lincolnshire and Norfolk are my favourite counties. I can't easily explain why I like Shropshire so much, save that beauty is in the eye of the beholder, but it was with particularly pleasant anticipation that I entered Shropshire one hazy morning, driving blissfully over the county boundary where the A5 crosses the A41, then turning first left on to a by-road my family and our bosom pals, the Tanguys, know well, it being a habit of ours, when making for the Severn Valley, to pull in at a tree-shaded verge hereabouts for a first picnic of the day. Jackie and I were always notorious amongst kith and kin for consuming the bulk of our picnics within forty-five minutes of leaving the house. Journeys make you hungry, however sedentary your mode of travel.

With the Wrekin prominent in the blue distance - heaving his forest fleece as Housman would have it - I crossed the M54 (looking haughtily down on the hurrying hordes below) and ran into Shifnal, passing a school where I had once arrived so late for the start of a half-marathon road race that the leading runners were already sprinting off into the distance before I could park the car. Not that it affected my performance, I always start at the back, content in the knowledge that matters can only improve: "Never knowingly overtaken", that's my motto.

Leaving Shifnal, westbound, there's always a sense

"... the pints we never sank, the girls we didn't meet, because they lived at the end of Mystery Street."

that you are swapping one landscape for another. The main road wanted to take me to Telford, but I wasn't having any of it. I escaped on to the B4379 as if to make for Bridgnorth. And Bridgnorth would have been my target had I not been waylaid by an old fashioned, Shropshire County Highways, cast-iron signpost at Brockton, pointing beguilingly down a by-road to Coalport. I must have passed that sign fifty times or more and always made the same inward vow to visit Coalport when the opportunity arose. Signposts are like metaphors for life: they are the routes we never take, the experience we eschew for whatever half-baked excuse springs to mind; they are the might-have-beens, the conversations we never had, the pints we never sank, the girls we didn't meet, because they lived at the end of Mystery Street.

So, true to the spirit of discovery inherent in this book, I finally took the trouble to turn right and was immediately glad I had, because it was an agreeable little road, passing farms and traversing the perimeter of a mellow brick wall protecting Brocton Court from vulgar gaze. It crossed the A442 , then ascended to reveal some distant hills which I took to be Brown Clee and Titterstone Clee. Then it swooped down towards the Severn through woods which smelled of wild garlic and past a farm advertising broad beans for sale, my favourite vegetable. A line of council houses quickly followed, and I was looking for a spot to turn before disillusion set in, when I came upon a magnificent china works with two splendid bottle kilns and, a little further on, a bridge spanning an inclined plane connecting two levels of an old canal. Fragments of memory came back to me. I was within the purlieus of the Ironbridge Gorge Museum and these industrial throwbacks were the Coalport China works, the Hay Incline and the Shropshire Canal respectively. What fun! I parked the Morgan and set off on foot to explore, coming also upon a footbridge over the Severn bearing a poignant memorial plaque to the fallen of the First World War. I was thoroughly

enamoured with the whole set up. Previously I had consciously avoided Ironbridge and its all singing all dancing heritage displays. Not because I have an aversion to the heritage industry, which has saved so much of high value for future generations to enjoy, but because I have a fond memory of a visit to Ironbridge in the Fifties as a child, and often, as you know, it is better not to go back. But on this early June morning the adrenalin was pumping, and I was making mental notes to return with all the family.

Walking along a restored section of canal, a few lines of Betjeman swam into my head, lines concerning Captain Webb, Webb the Dawley man, swimming along the old canal which carried the bricks to Lawley. The absence of inverted commas illustrates that I paraphrase from memory, but I'm sure you know the poem I mean, and can recite it as a party piece better than I. And those bottle kilns - gosh! As an A level art student I had a thing about bottle kilns, and did a painting of a landscape filled with them that helped me win the school's annual Art Prize, an irony not lost on me, given that I would have rather been in the First XV. To press home the point on Speech Day, I exhibited a painting depicting a set of rugger posts made up from paintbrush uprights and a human crossbar, dressed in sports kit and holding aloft the Art Prize. All very Magritte, I know, but I think they took the point!

I got back in the car and retraced my steps as far as the first road junction. Something made me turn right and I'm glad it did, because the road led down to a bridge over the Severn. 'One vehicle only at a time' it said, wise counsel (or should that be wise *council*), for the bridge had been erected in 1818. To me it looked almost as impressive as the original 'ironbridge' just upstream, and I was pleased to have come upon it by chance, and glad to know there were still surprises to be had in middle age.

Under sheer red sandstone cliffs I came to Bridgnorth. I derive perennial enjoyment from driving over the Severn

Coalbrookdale
Top left: Coalport Bridge
Lower left: The Hay Inclined Plane
Right: The China Works

into this characterful old town with its split personality of High and Low. I like the seed merchant's painted advert on the gable end of a building hard by the bridge, and the clifftop vista of High Town, book-ended by two disparate churches, the southernmost having been built to the designs of that ubiquitous genius of 18th century engineering, Thomas Telford. Parking by the riverbank in Low Town, I made my way to the Cliff Railway, a funicular that, in the words of the tourist bumph, 'has been transporting passengers up and down the 111ft sandstone cliffs between High and Low Towns since 1892'. Its survival is remarkable, and unique - I think - away from its coastal equivalents in seaside towns like Hastings, Saltburn and Lynmouth. Its origins stem from a typically Victorian impatience with the numerous flights of steps, most exceeding two hundred in number, which effected commerce between the two vertically distinct portions of the town. In an early essay in market research a local councillor estimated that over three thousand persons per day were making the laborious journey between High and Low and vice versa. Good business would evidently accrue to entrepreneurs prepared to fund the construction of a rail link.

George Newnes, the publisher who had already had experience with cliff railways at Lynton & Lynmouth in North Devon, had patented a form of inclined railway, and he became Chairman of the Bridgnorth project. Given its precipitous locale, construction demanded great care. Gravity was cheated by the filling and emptying of water tanks. Those familiar with Gerard Hoffnung's immortal comic tale of the bricklayer and his errant barrel of bricks will quite easily be able to grasp the theory involved. It's all a question of balance, and being no engineer, I must retire gracefully with my technical integrity intact at this point. Suffice it to say that, in 1944, hydraulic operating methods were usurped by electrical and a system employing rope and revolving drums. It's all 'smoke and mirrors' to me, but my lack of mechanical aplomb is more than compensated for by the sheer enjoyment I derived from the all too brief ride.

I paid my 70p for a return ticket, joined three other astronauts in one of the cars, and prepared myself for take off. The attendant closed the door, a bell rang portentously, and the car leapt into life, a rocket bound for another galaxy. Rising above the rooftops of Low Town, the car's wide windows offered grandstand views of the Severn, flowing with statesmanlike dignity beneath its cutwatered bridge. 'The finest view in all my kingdom', Charles I is reputed to have said of Bridgnorth, before it all went to his head. I might have been in Lyon, or Lauterbrunnen or Lisbon. John Betjeman likened the ascent to being lifted up to heaven. If only we could all ascend to the Pearly Gates by funicular it would be heavenly indeed.

The Cliff Railway - Bridgnorth

We passed the other car coming down. At the top a man let us out and we drifted into High Town. Frances Moore of *Old Moore's Almanac* fame was born in Bridgnorth in 1657. Could he have predicted how modern road transport would blight his home town? Such a gorgeous High Street, so much traffic! A brewery dray was delivering to one of the numerous public houses, restricting incoming traffic to a thrombotic throng. All my attempts to find a dignified viewpoint from which to photograph the handsome arched and half-timbered 17th century town hall, which straddles High Street, were thwarted by an ugly miasma of parked and moving vehicles. Here, I thought, was a High Street crying out for pedestrianisation, though aware of the dangers inherent in such a course. Simply banning traffic can have an adverse effect: a thoroughfare can lose its vigour; too much space can be exposed between the buildings which flank the street unless something positive is provided to fill the vacuum. To pedestrianise or not to pedestrianise, that's the dilemma. Personally I'd ban all vehicles built after 1963: 'between the Lady Chatterley ban and the Beatles' first LP'. Though there would have to be a loophole for my Morgan and other stylish equivalents of later manufacture constructed to precepts of high aesthetic virtue as judged by a quango of experts headed by me on a large retainer.

Perambulating High Town I assimilated the finer details of its architecture, particularly taken with the ugly Victorian market hall of blue and yellow brick. Though a blatant intruder amidst fine Georgian neighbours, it lacked the brutalising effect that a 20th century building would have impacted on the scene. In Telford's St Mary Magdalene's churchyard I came upon an iron gravestone commemorating the ironmaking Hazeldine family.

The streets were filling with shoppers. I found myself behind three lady members of the Shropshire Obstructive-Walking Society. Tactically they were brilliant, a credit to their hobby. Each time I attempted to overtake them they closed ranks and forced me back. At a guess (because, obviously, I lacked the sophisticated measuring equipment officially employed on race days) they were averaging no more than two hundred yards an hour. What impressed me most was their ability to talk, window-shop, and ignore all other passers-by simultaneously. By the time we reached Woolworths I'd learnt that Graham was in Kidderminster having his appendix taken out, that Ken and Brenda were on a coach tour in Yugoslavia, that ninety pence was extortionate for a lettuce of such size, and that Barbara could argue 'til the cows came home but that shade of blue didn't suit her.

The High Town station, Bridgnorth

The road to Highley plays hopscotch with the Severn Valley Railway and passes the entrance to Daniel's Mill, an 18th century water mill featuring a huge waterwheel located in attractive juxtaposition with a high redbrick viaduct. Lovingly restored to grind wholemeal flour, the mill is open to visitors on Wednesday and weekend afternoons throughout the summer. The countryside is so lovely and innocent that it comes as something of a shock to discover that there was once much industrial activity in the area. At Eardington there was an ironworks ingeniously linked to the Severn by an underground canal. Ever more astonishingly, Highley lay at the heart of a coalfield, a coalfield, moreover, worked until as recently as 1969 when Alveley Mine was closed by the NCB on account of geological difficulties, a frequent euphemism employed by management to obfuscate their often inept handling of the economics of coal mining.

Highley's village sign immediately gives clue to its industrial past, being in the form of a colliery headstock wheel. It's a long, straggling village featuring several eras of housing style, a number unmistakably being of Coal Board origin. Some temporary traffic lights brought me to a halt by a long row of terraced cottages called Clee View. It did not take much imagination to picture colliers emerging from each doorway on their way to a fresh shift at the mine. In latter years, when the pithead had shifted across the Severn, from the original Highley mine to the new shaft at Alveley, the men crossed the river in punts to reach their subterranean workplace. Nearer the heart of the village, I came upon more terraced backstreets, one called Coronation Street which looked as though it belonged much further to the north. In the main street a sculptured clock depicts a miner about to descend into the bowels of the earth in a cage. Coming in and out of shops, several elderly men looked as though the experience had been a familiar daily routine.

At the far end of the village I turned left and followed a steep lane down towards the river, coming down to earth with a bump at the Severn Valley Railway's picturesque Highley station. Midweek, out of high season, trains are few and far between, but it is this very lack of intensity, which evokes a more true to life period branchline atmosphere than manifested at busier times, when hordes of tourists and train buffs descend - on what is one of Britain's most popular preserved railways - in droves. With only the signalman and a young porter within hailing distance, and they self-absorbed in authentic duties, I was exquisitely left to my own devices.

I imagined that H. F. S. Morgan would have enjoyed being there beside me, and perhaps Peter Morgan, his son, as well. For a family so closely associated with cars and motoring, railways provided a relaxation, and a sizeable Bassett Lowke O gauge layout occupied space in their Malvern Link home. Parked beside the old level crossing gate on the branch which had led to Highley mine, my V8 looked resplendent, and almost organic. 'Perhaps because the frames are built of ash', I mused, getting slightly carried away. The first Morgan four wheelers went into production in 1936, and my car bore all the family traits of its ancestry.

Time passed against a melodic soundtrack of birdsong: the hoot of a woodpigeon, a piping blackbird, a fluting finch, chattering magpies, a cackling jay, whilst somewhere in the back of beyond an industrious woodpecker sent a muffled ostinato rhythm ricocheting through the woods. Down over the tiled rooftops of riverbank cottages and the Ship Inn, I could see the Severn, caramel-coloured and uncharacteristically sluggish, flowing insouciantly by. Two middle-aged men (and with a jolt I realised that I could now hold my own in such company) wandered down the lane discussing England's start in the Old Trafford Test and anticipating a cool pint in the pub. Presently a bell rang in the signal

Coal mining monument, Highley

Deep panting train - the Severn Valley Railway

box and some wires beside me rustled conspiratorially in their pulleys. A signal in the middle distance clanked down from its 'go no further' horizontal to a more obliging 'pass friend' angle of forty-five degrees. From way down the valley the sound of a labouring train came on the breeze. A whistle shrieked, and, in the due course of branchline time, what Rupert Brooke once so eloquently described as a 'deep panting train' hoved into view, passed my shady vantage point, slowed to exhange the section token with the signalman who'd come down in shirtsleeves from his timber eyrie, and groaned to a halt at Highley station.

"Highley, Highley," shouted the boy porter, echoing generations of his professional progenitors since the opening of the line in 1862. One or two doors slammed and one or two ramblers decanted themselves and their haversacks out on to the low platform. A sort of trance-like silence ensued, a tableau briefly frozen. Then, as if suddenly conscious of the march of time, the porter proudly blew his whistle, the engine answered affirmatively, and the whole ensemble puffed purposefully away up the valley to repeat the whole performance by popular demand at Hampton Loade.

Whilst waiting for the train, I had scribbled some nodal points relevant to the next stage of my itinerary on a scrap of paper. Had someone glanced over my shoulder they would have thought I was dabbling in poetry:

Billingsley, Deuxhill, Middleton Scriven
Walkerslow, Baytree, Cleobury North
Ditton Priors, Tugford, Diddlebury
Corfton, Craven Arms, Stokesay Castle

Of course one need look no further than the first line of A. E. Housman's *A Shropshire Lad* to find first rate poetry inspired by this landscape:

From Clee to heaven the beacon burns

and there was Clee - Brown Clee and Titterstone Clee - horizoning the way ahead as I negotiated a labyrinthine sequence of by-roads cutting across the grain of the countryside in a westerly direction. Shaking free of Highley, I swooped down through a tunnel of trees to where the road fords Borle Brook. There's nothing I like better than a good deep ford: the potential to create

The ford at Borle Brook

spectacular waves and sudden silvery explosions of spray. Not being familiar with this one, however, it was with due circumspection that I drove slowly through it. A helpful gauge was provided, capable of measuring depths of up to six feet of water. On this occasion, despite the wetness of the season, it was through a modest nine inches of water that the Morgan rumbled, not without an element of regret.

I must be getting soft in my old age I thought as I accelerated away up a steepish slope to join the B4363 at Billingsley. There was a pub on the corner called the Cape of Good Hope. Somewhere I'd read that the landlord here had been instrumental in kick-starting the search for coal in the vicinity in the mid 19th century. Billingsley Colliery had stood alongside the inn and a mineral line was built along the banks of Borle Brook to take coal down to the Severn Valley Railway and thence the hungry carpet factory furnaces of Kidderminster. Billingsley mine closed in 1921 but, had I had time to look, I might still have come upon some small spoil tips, the remains of an inclined plane and sundry brick buildings of mining heritage.

At Deuxhill I turned left at a signpost beckoning to The Down and Middleton Scriven. From time to time I caught glimpses up ahead of Brown Clee. At Middleton a man looked up from painting a fence and gave me a cheery wave, and I liked to think that my passing had enlivened a dull task. Rounding a tight bend and plunging into a dark tree covered cutting, I came upon a JCB blocking the road. It seemed to be engaged in clearing a drain and was shovelling quantities of silt into a lorry. There was no way round, but the two drivers cheerfully reversed their vehicles to a provident widening of the road to let me pass. I was traversing a remote tract of country and encountered no other traffic for mile after mile. Sequestered farms punctuated my progress. Mud on the road suggested that their tractors were its most frequent users. The Morgan, though, was gobbling up the miles, and moreover I was feeling hungry and ready for lunch. Valerian spilled from cottage gardens as I skirted Cleobury North. At a crossroads a man cried out to an invisible friend: "Hey, look at this," and I left him gaping in admiration as I let the V8 rip and accelerated away in a cloud of dust. Slowly but surely the Morgan was beginning to impress its character on its new driver.

My chosen route now skirted the brackeny hemline of Brown Clee. It is a beautiful hill, seventeen hundred and something feet high at its summit, though I was so close to its precipitous flank that my view of the top was curtailed. A metaphor for friendship there, I thought, the closer you are to someone the less you see their true character. Another collision was narrowly avoided, in the shape of a 4x4 being driven by one of those otherwise perfectly demure women who, as soon as they get behind the wheel of one, become charged people, acting as if they were charged with the task of delivering aid parcels to remote and ravaged communities in the Third World. I waved cheerfully to acknowledge our mutual escape, she pressed on, deeper and deeper into the Belgian Congo.

Over my right shoulder I caught glimpses of what I guessed was The Wrekin, now seen from the opposite side to my early morning views of it, but a nervous little voice kept telling me to cut out the scenic tour and keep my eyes on the road. It began to feel as if I was on a computer game in a seaside arcade with hazards being thrown at me round every corner. In Tugford I stopped to look at the map and was reassured to find myself still on course. The road had dropped me down into Corve Dale and there was less now a sense of wildness and more a comfortable landscape of agricultural well being. I passed the motte & bailey remains of Corfham Castle and would have liked to have gone in search of Rosamund's Well but for the rumbling protestations of my stomach. Diddlebury seemed positively suburban and the B4368 evinced an almost motorway-like intensity of traffic compared to the quiet lanes behind me. So, temporarily returned to the dubious bosom of civilization, I made fast work of the five miles to Craven Arms, eschewed the all too tempting aroma of fish & chips therein, and pulled up in the car park at Stokesay Castle just on the point of noon.

Silent noon? Not quite! On the neighbouring hillside a motorised shepherd on a 'quad' was noisily moving his flock to pastures new. The sheep still made the same idyllic bleating sounds as yore, but I doubted if their high-tech keeper would be lunching in the shade of a hedgerow with a flagon of cider brought to him by a dewy-eyed girl like the untrustworthy Hireling Shepherd in Rossetti's Pre-Raphaelite painting.

Stokesay Castle, a 13th century Marcher fortress, is cared for by English Heritage and their approach is commendably under-played. If there are ghosts here, they remain undisturbed by the worst atrocities of tourism. The result is a haunt of ancient peace, if that's not a contradiction in the case of a building built to deter aggressors. I paid my entry fee, but turned down the kind offer of an audio pack to guide me round the castle. I'd been there, done that, on a previous occasion and, interesting and informative

The gate house, Stokesay Castle

as the tape had been, this time I wanted just to mooch about, soaking up the resonance of the ancient stonework and half-timbering. Besides, I self-consciously didn't want to look as daft as all the other visitors who were wandering about with the hand held audio machines held to their ears as if speaking to their stock-brokers on a mobile phone.

I made a bee-line for the cafe and purchased a salmon sandwich and a slice of caramel and apple pie with a bottle of sparkling mineral water (which I was glad to see had been sourced locally at Moreton-on-Lugg and not the Scottish Highlands or the French Alps) to slake my thirst. A table was free in the garden and I carried my lunch over to it on a tray. It proved a very pleasant interlude. Swallows ducked and dived over the ancient rooftops, bees droned in the flowerbeds, a lady watercolourist worked demurely at her sketch pad. From an adjacent table a middle-aged blonde regarded me out of the corner of her eye, wondering, perhaps, at my busy note-taking. The length of her hair was perhaps a tad too long for a woman of her age. There was grey in it, and though undeniably attractive, this gave her a slightly sinister air, perfect for a potential murderess in a Ngaio Marsh crime novel. She would start with me if she could read this, I thought. She and her male companion, who might once have made a handsome couple, sat silently across their table from each other, immersed in their own thoughts, lively conversation no longer the lingua franca of matrimony.

Finished eating, I went walkabout, exploring the refreshingly cool, subfusc, and largely unfurnished, interiors before ascending on to the battlemented tower for a bird's eye view of the grounds and surrounding countryside. I might have been a Marcher lord, scanning the landscape for potential enemies, hand on the hilt of my sword in case a few scoundrels heads required severing from their bodies. Or I might have been watching to see her ladyship depart on horseback for Ludlow for new rolls of muslin before dallying deliciously with her maid. Swashbuckling down the steps like Errol Flynn, I contented myself with a swim around the moat, a virtual swim that is, because the moat has been drained and turned into a charming path through which you walk between burgeoning banks of wild flowers. Not that I wouldn't have preferred there still to be a moat. The presence of water enhances everything. Modern developers recognise this: that's why canals are proving a popular ally in the regeneration of inner cities.

A pre-conditioned family man, I was unable to leave Stokesay without visiting the souvenir shop and dipping into my pocket; though I must say

English Heritage shops are invariably filled with items of at least some intrinsic value, practical or otherwise. I bought a nice little Everyman book called *Local Heroes* by Peter Ashley, an enamel badge, and two wooden rulers with the kings and queens of England printed chronologically on the back - rulers, get it! The friendly assistant provided me with a large plastic carrier bag in which to carry these wares, explaining: "We're out of the intermediate size of bag." 'Aren't we all,' I thought, and went off whistling through the churchyard. On the road into Craven Arms I passed a new much vaunted visitor centre called Explore the Secret Hills. It all looked very high tech and inviting, but I had read their leaflet and always make a rule of avoiding places which use the adjective 'fascinating' more than three times in their publicity material.

Some delightful by-roads carried me cross country to Bishop's Castle. I had thought of going via Clun, but felt that the day was already running away with me, and there was much ground I intended to travel yet. I went by way of Hopesay and Lydbury and saw a big house standing smugly across the valley of the River Kemp called Walcot, wishing that I had in my collection a copy of John Betjeman's *Shell Guide to Shropshire* with which to elaborate. Later I discovered that it was the home of Clive of India, and that the lake I glimpsed in front of it had been enlarged by French prisoners captured during the Napoleonic Wars. Scratch the surface, retire a few paces, and see what happens!

All that I knew about Bishop's Castle was that it once lay at the end of an eccentric and impecunious branch line railway and that it was the location of a wonderful home brew pub called The Three Tuns. What I discovered was a small hillside town, not unlike Hay-on-Wye. Certainly it boasted a good few secondhand bookshops, and, I sensed, leanings towards the New Age. Parking spaces were at a premium, and I had to circumnavigate the centre twice before finding a space on the fringe of town.

It was two-thirty, and I was just in time for a half at The Three Tuns. The bar was post-prandially quiet, but the muzak a tad intrusive in an establishment of such long pedigree. When will publicans learn that the only soundtrack they need is the hubbub of voices or, alternatively, a John Cage like silence in which to savour one's ale and mull over one's misfortunes? I took my drink into a diminutive, pavilion-like annex overlooking the brewery's handsome brick tower, and sipped it appreciatively. The pub boasted a rather nice line in oval beer mats and I surreptitiously smuggled one out with me. It wouldn't be the best public house I'd encounter on my journeys, but any concern surviving in

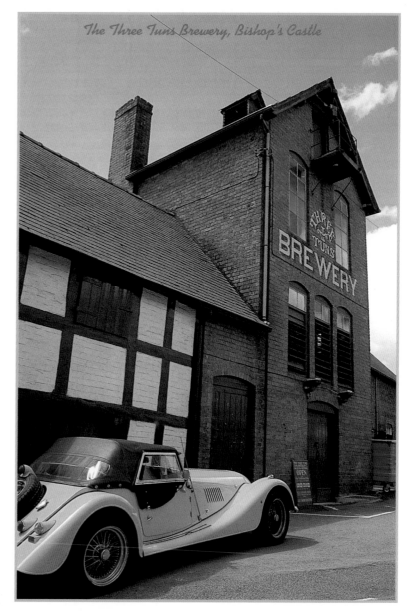

The Three Tuns Brewery, Bishop's Castle

business since the 17th century deserved credit and a toast to continued longevity. I don't imagine Wetherspoons and Firkins and Tom Cobleigh will be around in 2402! Out of fairness, I should add that Bishop's Castle boasts another brewery in the Six Bells on Church Street, and that if I hadn't been driving I would have reported on this as well.

Being a weekday, I was unable to visit either the House on Crutches museum of local history and rural life, or the Rail & Transport Museum, much of which is devoted to the town's notoriously unremunerative railway which spent sixty nine out of its seventy years in existence in the hands of the receiver. Sauntering round the steeply sloping streets, I overheard the owner of a furniture shop explaining to a lady customer that his chairs were made of ash, "just like a Morgan car." Serendipity? Or had he wistfully watched me climbing the steep High Street and longed for an open top and an equally open road in exchange for the confines of his workshop?

Inevitably, I was drawn into a secondhand bookshop bearing the imaginative name of Autolycus. Shakespearians and A Level English Literature students will recall the character of Autolycus, the pedlar, in *A Winter's Tale*, self-described as 'a snapper-up of unconsidered trifles'. The shop had a fine selection of stock, nicely presented and not unfairly priced, but I was still in a post-Hay mindset of denial. A nice clean edition of Robert Gittings's *Coming Down the Seine* had me sorely tempted though, and if the shop hadn't suddenly filled I would have got my money out of my wallet, for if I am on my own in a bookshop I can't avoid feeling that it is bad manners to leave without purchasing at least one volume. As if to underline this, outside again in the street, I eavesdropped on shopkeeper's bemoaning the lack of trade. Feeling pangs of guilt for not contributing to the community coffers, I hurried back to the car and made for the hills.

Mary Webb called Bishop's Castle 'Mallard's Keep'. Not that Mary Webb means much to many people now. Virago revived her Shropshire novels twenty years or more ago, but the authoress (who was once thought so highly of that Stanley Baldwin and John Buchan and G. K. Chesterton were eagerly recruited to write forewords to the illustrated editions of her work posthumously published by Jonathan Cape in the early 1930s) seems to have fallen back into the black hole of indifference where the general public are concerned. Jackie and I collected these books avidly, as much, from my perspective, for Norman Hepple's and Rowland Hilder's evocative illustrations, as the story

The Autolycus Bookshop, Bishop's Castle

lines, which were possibly too female in content to fully hold my attention, though I remember enjoying *Seven For a Secret* immensely. Probably - knowing me as well as I do - because it featured a railway journey. And not just any railway journey but, as far as I could make out, given Mary Webb's habit (derived from her literary hero, Thomas Hardy, I suspect) of creating her own topographical Shropshire, but a train ride shared by the heroine, Gillian Lovekin, and hero, Robert Rideout, along the Bishop's Castle Railway to Craven Arms, alias 'The Junction':

'There, about a mile away, between two hills of bare larches, which shone golden in the afternoon sunlight, was a puff of white smoke - the train.'

Once aboard the train, true love was following a typically convoluted course:

'With a wild and gloomy expression he turned his back on her, and did not look at her again until they had passed the three wayside stations set in the woods, and were nearing the Junction.'

Eaton, Plowden and Horderley I imagine she referred to, and here I was driving through Plowden and there were those woods and hills of bare larches and a little bridge spanning the River Onny.

Climbing up to the Long Mynd

An acute angle faces the motorist who elects to turn eastbound from the A489 on to the by-road which follows the backbone of the Long Mynd, referred to in the Mary Webb canon as Wilderhope. Without the benefit of power steering, I had to effect the turn in three manoeuvres, all the while occupying alarming portions of the main road. Matters were exacerbated by the appearance of another sports car - its open top revealing an elderly couple out for a spin - coming down off the hills and, for what seemed an eternity, I was 'an accident waiting to happen' had any fast moving vehicle zoomed by on the main road. So it was with a sigh of relief that I got underway and began to ascend through lush banks of bracken, rising above the treetops of the East Onny valley on to the whaleback heights of the Long Mynd, a plateau clothed in heather and blueberry, Britain's southernmost grouse moor.

The Long Mynd inspired another novelist, or at least a writer of children's adventure stories. Malcolm Saville's own children were evacuated here at the outbreak of the Second World War and the setting inspired their father to begin his sequence of Lone Pine tales with *Mystery at Witchend*. The sky had been darkening ominously since leaving Stokesay and now it began to rain, softly at first but with a growing intensity which made me pull in and hastily put the hood up. The rain irritated me, and yet I can remember when I loved rain, not to mention wind and cold and frost and snow. Middle age had me under surveillance. I craved warmth and sunlight for my ageing bones.

A sudden noise woke me from maudlin thoughts of mortality, and I focused on the road as a three-wheeled sports car in racing green screeched round an approaching corner and roared away down the road in front of me. It contained two serious looking motorists in caps and goggles. Nonplussed, I swung right impetuously, not entirely sure if I wanted to go right, but glad to get away from the possibility of a chance encounter with real enthusiasts who might heartily wish to exchange jargon and data, and thereby expose me as a fraud: a man with a Morgan who doesn't know his camshaft from his carburettor.

As it transpired, I'd made the turn I wanted. What I wasn't prepared for was the astonishingly unnerving steepness of the road I'd selected blithely on the map. I might have looked more closely at the huddled contours and the double arrows indicative of a gradient steeper than 1 in 5. Actually, 1 in 2 might have been more accurate in this instance. I have recurring nightmares about rolling backwards uncontrollably in a car, and here I seemed faced with the prospect in all too vivid reality. I put my foot to the floor. This seemed to be exactly what the Morgan - or rather its V8 Rover engine - had been waiting for. It was like letting an impatient hound off a lead. The car bounded forward with a lurch and shot uphill. It's not my style to exaggerate for effect. So you must take it as gospel when I tell you that only the Morgan's rear wheels remained, at that point, on the tarmac. Hands glued to the steering wheel, eyes welded to the road, I hung on for dear life, assuming that attack was the best form of defence, and that only my continued forward progress could prevent me from a terrible end.

The V8 was enjoying itself hugely. "At last some real motoring," it seemed to be chuckling to itself, "no more of this spinsterly pottering about on by-roads!" I suppose I had gone a few hundred yards, and was beginning to relax a little myself, feeling that perhaps I'd missed my vocation, and that I should enter myself for the Shelsley Walsh Hill Trials at the earliest convenience, when I chanced to look to my left, seeing with a fresh wave of pure undiluted funk - nothing! Nothing, that is, but lowering cloud and a limitless sky. My worst fears were confirmed, the Morgan and I had taken off, we were in mid air. There appeared to be no other rational explanation. I felt exactly as one might feel in the open cockpit of a small aeroplane. I expected the radio at any moment to cackle into life: "Bandits, twelve o'clock, Tally Ho, Leader, Tally Ho." And there they were above me, coming out of the cloud, Heinkels or Junkers, bearing down on me with malice aforethought and death staring out of their gunsights.

My mind flew back to all those *Victor* and *Wizard* comics I'd avidly

consumed as an eight year old. This was no time for cold feet, there was a war to be won. Instinctively, I wrenched the driving wheel clockwise, planning to get above the enemy planes and swoop down on them from their blind spot. What actually happened next was that I found myself looking at a fresh stretch of road, reassuringly less steep. Moreover the bend I'd just unconsciously negotiated had taken me away from the road's high ledge and there was thymy grass, bracken and of all things sheep comfortingly beside me again on both sides. And the enemy planes? Oh they were just two gliders freshly taken off from the adjoining premises of the Midland Gliding Club. "Relax you fool," I told myself, and eased my foot off the accelerator: "Less of the melodramatics, you've two pretty nurses to take to the NAFFI dance tonight. Roger and out."

That run across the old Port Way would have been idyllic in sunlight. In the rain, with the three wipers essaying a mad Busby Berkley dance routine across the windscreen, and in the post-trauma, adrenalin-pumping gratitude of my cancelled appointment with death, it had the insubstantial and amorphous atmosphere of a moonscape. Gradually my confidence returned. By Boiling Well I had to toss a coin: heads Church Stretton and the potential of comforting coffee cake; tails Ratlinghope, Stipperstones and more seat of the pants stuff. My trusty threepenny piece fell heads. Newly empowered, I turned right, I can have cake when I'm sixty and bore the socks off my grandchildren with tales of motoring daring do.

I pulled in and consulted the map. The rain beat down on the hood in a rhythm reminiscent of nights spent in wet tents on the Duke of Edinburgh's Award. The road ahead lay across an area called Wild Moor, a pretty accurate description from what I could make out through the wet side windows. After my adventure in the air, I had now to come to terms with water. A wild moorland sea stretched into infinity, an ocean swell of sheep and heather and whinberry. This was the country of Mary Webb's *Golden Arrow* and *Gone to Earth*; the latter made into a film by my cinematic heroes Michael Powell and Emeric Pressburger. The film-making caravanserai settled on Much Wenlock in 1949 to shoot the film - Powell and Pressburger (aka 'The Archers') always preferring to use authentic locations for their work. Somewhat inappropriately, the American starlet Jennifer Jones, was given the lead role of Mary Webb's Shropshire waif, Hazel Woodus, indubitably because she was currently the amour of the all American

The old engine shed, Snailbeach

producer, David O. Selznick.

The road bore down on Ratlinghope, which Mary Webb called 'the small huddled village of Slepe'. I followed it, leaving the moors behind, passing into a more convivial landscape of farms and cottages. I slowed down to let a horse and rider negotiate a way past me on the narrow lane. The horsewoman had her face set cheerfully into the rain and the wilderness beyond, patently deriving excitement from the elements. At Bridges I came upon a Youth Hostel housed in an old school. I crossed the East Onny river and let the car have its head again to ascend another steep hill. The rain was really heavy now and the presence of a sign for a farm called Squilver seemed almost onomatopoeic.

In some respects, the Wagnerian elements suited Stiperstones. Fifteen hundred feet above sea level the heathery moorlands had given way to rocky outcrops, a sinister haunted landscape where the Devil is said to have strode about, flinging boulders in a fit of pique. One really needs to be on foot to do justice to such a landscape, to delve into its legends, to savour its brooding atmosphere. And as, by definition, this is a motoring book, I'll have to leave you short-changed and wondering. But what I can tell you, is that, in descending into Pennerley, I was reminded of nothing so much as of Cornwall. Not, of course, the pretty Cornwall of the calendars and coffee table books, but industrial Cornwall, where the detritus of the china clay and tin mining industries leaves permanent (and quite often rather attractive, in a sultry kind of way) scars on the landscape. Pennerley brought to mind Roche on Bodmin Moor; and my instincts were reliable, for this was south-west Shropshire's ore mining region from probably Roman times right up until the 1950s.

In spite of the rain, I responded to the urge to abandon the car and go in search of industrial archaeological remains: ruined engine houses, ivy-clad chimneys, mine-workers cottages; all as Cornish as a Ginster's pasty. Lead, copper, zinc and barytes were all extracted in the vicinity of Snailbeach and Pennerley. The production of local lead peaked in the latter half of the 19th century. Cheap imports, like those which effectively caused the demise of the British mining industry brought about a slow demise. Snailbeach Mine was the last to close. The bulk of its output was conveyed to the world beyond on a 2ft 4ins gauge railway at one time managed by that stalwart of independent railways, Colonel Stephens, a railway hero of the 'small is beautiful but unlikely to ever pay' school, a civil engineer by learning, but

Lead mine remains, Snailbeach

one imbued with poetry and art, doubtless because his father was the Pre-Raphaelite chronicler and artist, F. G. Stephens.

The local authority has cleaned up the site and provided interpretive boards. You park by the public conveniences and trudge up a steep track to the mine. It is all very atmospheric and intriguing, and, with no one about on this wet afternoon, I was able to rummage at will, empathizing with the miners who worked eight hour shifts by candlelight to earn twenty-two shillings a week. On the 6th of March 1895 seven of them were killed when the cage in which they were lowered into the bowels of the earth plummeted to the bottom of the shaft after the winding rope snapped. I couldn't imagine how seven men could have squeezed into such a tiny space. The winding wheel has been restored, and stands eloquently silhouetted against a backdrop of silent woods. My feet got wet in the undergrowth. Rails still run into the engine shed. I peered through its cobwebby windows to see if some ancient locomotive still lurked inside like Puff the Magic Dragon, wanting only coal and water to make it steam again. No such luck, just some rusty machinery. I walked back down to the car in nostalgic vein.

I did not enjoy the drive to Shrewsbury. Minsterley reintroduced me to the 21st Century. We did not appear to have much in common. I suppose the rain and the road traffic had an adverse effect on my subjectivity, but at that moment I just thought how miserably most of us live now, in ugly streets of ugly houses, made uglier by the incessant passing of ugly cars and ugly lorries. And this ugliness rubs off on our demeanour and outlook, and makes us ugly too; brash and vulgar, self-seeking and self-absorbed. We are not good at building cathedrals any more, we are good at building retail parks and industrial estates, and the tourist industry would not need to exist if we did not all have a desperate craving to escape from the ugliness we had surrounded ourselves with.

Shrewsbury was emptying. The tea time tide picked me up, carried me through the town centre, and deposited me in the only car parking space available by the Abbey. It was not a bad place to land.

High the vanes of Shrewsbury gleam
Islanded in Severn Stream;

Thus wrote A. E. Housman, and with almost topographical truth, for only a narrow neck of land by the railway station prevents this most beautiful of large English towns from being located on a true island. Alight from a train at the splendidly Tudoresque railway station, and you can take yourself on a two mile circular towpath walk of great beauty and fascination. And short of a Morgan, the train really is the best way of making your way to Shrewsbury, as did Neville Cardus on the 1st May, 1912 in a third class compartment from Manchester London Road, a compartment 'overpowering with that odour of stuffed seats and padding which is peculiar to railways'. In his *Autobiography*, the great music critic and cricket writer recalled 'the refreshment of air when I pulled the leather strap and let down a pane on which was printed "Non-Smoker"'. According to the flyleaf, on which I habitually note the place of purchase, I obtained my copy of the Cardus autobiography for thirty-five pence in Rye in 1981. It was a good buy, and keeps an honoured place in the glass-fronted bookcase which contains my most prized books. Cardus and I share a passion for music and the old Manchester of *The Guardian* and the Free Trade Hall, where I am glad to be able to remember both Barbirolli and Boult conducting. Cardus was travelling to Shrewsbury to take up the post of Assistant Cricket Coach at Shrewsbury School. His account of the railway journey, from a Manchester whose endless streets 'stretched away in a static lean dreary hopelessness', through Cheshire countryside where 'evening light fell on cows standing still in the meadows', via Crewe where he watched 'porters hauling bags and cases and crates and noisy milk-cans out of the luggage van', to a Shrewsbury where he walked up from the station 'past the Library with the Darwin statue outside' is one of my favourite descriptions of a railway ride. That reference to the aroma of a railway carriage is echoed in Philip Larkin's poem *The Whitsun Weddings* and that line about 'the reek of buttoned carriage-cloth'. But it is another poet who one must pay homage to in Shrewsbury, and that, of course, is Wilfred Owen, whose father was a Traffic Superintendent at Shrewsbury station. See then, how all these strands connect, and watch me walking purposefully across the English Bridge, mentally accompanied by dead poets and journalists as shop assistants from Dixons and building society clerks from the Alliance & Leicester go past in the opposite direction, home for tea and Neighbours via a quick cocktail in the *Cuticle & Nail Clipper* or some equally anodyne all day dive.

I had forgotten how agreeable Shrewsbury was, though now, naturally, there are far more restaurants and bars than there were twenty-five years ago when Jackie and I were thrilled to eat gammon & egg at the Berni Inn, thinking ourselves the height of sophistication, and holding, I imagine, an unbeaten record for devouring a meal in just eight minutes so as to ensure that we did not miss *Raveningham Hall* steaming through Shrewsbury station on a return special from Chester. Now, however, there is such a plethora of bars, brasseries, bistros and sandwich shops that I am convinced if I lived and worked in Shrewsbury I would be twice the girth. Oddly enough, I almost did once find employment in Shrewsbury, in circumstances I can't totally recall, save that I motored over for an interview with an advertising agency who wanted an account executive. After an agreeable interview it became apparent to both parties that I was never likely to be able to *account* for anything, whilst any resemblance I might have had to an *executive* was purely coincidental.

Like most British towns and cities, Shrewsbury dies a death at tea-time. We may embrace greater Europe, but we seem incapable of sustaining life and commerce beyond a five-thirty curfew. In a town of similar size and status on the continent I would have come upon a congenial pavement cafe from which to watch the world go by. Instead, I walked past Darwin's statue in the opposite direction to Neville Cardus, and found myself on a footbridge called The Dana spanning the tracks of the railway station from which I could hear muffled announcements of arrival and departure. If you know your Housman you will know that Shrewsbury Gaol overlooks the railway station, for the ninth poem in *A Shropshire Lad* concerns the unfortunates who are to be hung in the morning in Shrewsbury gaol but who cannot sleep for the noise of the trains. No hangings now, though the prison's gaunt Victorian facade can still send shivers down the most guiltless spine. Some steps led me swiftly down to the riverbank. Momentarily disorientated by the direction of the current, I fancied I should be heading downstream to find my way back to the English Bridge. Beneath the station, whose long platforms stretched out across the river, I encountered a chorus of pigeons humming in the gloom of the girders. A lovely, if rather weedgrown, river path, overlooked by elegant Georgian houses on one side and the rather ramshackle premises of the local football club's Gay Meadow ground on the other, carried me back to where I came from. I was happy to be on that reach of the river famous in footballing circles for the antics of the groundsman whose habit it was to retrieve balls hoofed loftily into the river by desperate centre-backs by means of a coracle.

The previous winter I had attended a concert in Shrewsbury Abbey of music by Moeran, Finzi, McCunn and other neglected British composers. The performers were an amateur orchestra, but made up for in enthusiasm what they lacked in expertise. I remember the brass being particularly effective in the Moeran *Symphony*. During the interval, I joined much of the audience in a walk across the road to the nearest available public conveniences, noting on the way, an attractive bistro called The Peach Tree, and it was to this establishment, trawled from my increasingly 'fished-out' memory bank, that I made my way on this rainy June evening, requesting and being shown to, 'a table for one', and enjoying a dish of creamy carbonara in the company of theatre-going couples: they anticipating an evening of drama, me reflecting on a packed day of numerous literary and musical encounters. Bubbling to the surface, like the effervescence in the Stella Artois glinting in its glass beside me, came a line from Wilfred Owen, not my favourite one about bugles calling from sad shires, but the one at the end of *The Send Off* about 'half-known roads' - it seemed somehow appropriate.

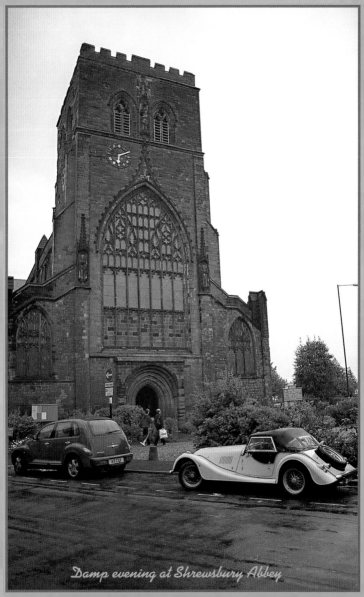

Damp evening at Shrewsbury Abbey

Roaring over the reservoir - Blithfield

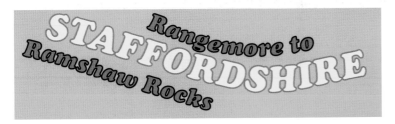

I did not have far to go to commence my exploration of Staffordshire. Just across the farmyard in fact. Farmyard's a tad misleading - since our long-time neighbour, Harold Salt, died a year or so back, the house has been empty, the milking parlour silent, and the old routine of cattle coming and going an absent echo. Small of stature, large of spirit, Harold had never married. The story went that his sweetheart had been killed in a road accident. It did not do to pry. His abrasive demeanour concealed just more layers of millstone grit. But he had every right to spit in the face of a world that had short-changed him. He lived rhythmically with the seasons. Early to bed and early to rise. Time wasn't measured by Greenwich, more by the moment when a beast was ready for market or the hay ready to cut. Going to market was his biggest adventure, and he'd chuckle with pride when informing - with no false modesty - that his beasts had weighed-in the heaviest that day. And on such occasions we'd hear him celebrating through the adjoining wall with a bottle or two of barley malt and a bit of a sing song to himself.

Unsullied by proprietary fertilizers, Harold's fields - all individually carrying names bestowed upon them generations back - played host to a botanist's playground of wild flowers. When Tamar was little it was our daily chore to help Harold see his thirteen cows safely down Cuckoo Cage Lane after milking. The arrival of the tanker was another rhythm in our day. When the Government disbanded the Milk Marketing Board the new private company didn't consider the milk of thirteen well contented cows worth collecting and the small herd was sold. Nothing was ever really the same again. He dabbled in fattening stock and tended his garden until cancer got him. He didn't tell anyone until the pain became unbearable. We didn't see him go downhill. He died the day after they took him into hospital. We wished fervently that he had died in his barn.

Rangemore is an estate village built on the profits of brewing. We have lived on its outskirts, but within its postal address, for almost twenty years. Located on the Needwood Forest plateau, two hundred and fifty feet above the Trent Valley, we have a horizon of power stations, as indigenous to the Trent as castles to the Rhine and chateaux to the Loire. 'Town' was four miles away and pretty much stayed there until Bass discovered that they could make more from property development than beer. Tamar, though not Eden, remembers fields where Morrisons and Currys and the Living Well Health Club now stand in all their greedy glory. But we feel safe on our hilltop - for the time being.

Sometimes disappointment can come from unsuspected directions. To get down into the valley we have to skirt an ancient hill called Battlestead. Beautifully bald and grazed by sheep, it had an almost downland atmosphere about it - Sussex transmuted to Staffordshire. Then the new National Forest paid the landowner to plant trees all over it, an unbelievably insensitive act of environmental despoilation, no less crass than the property developers. So, you see, sometimes you can know a county - or at least your home turf part of it - too well, it being far better to swan about landscapes like a stranger in paradise, making glib assumptions, and purring contentedly at unsolicited views.

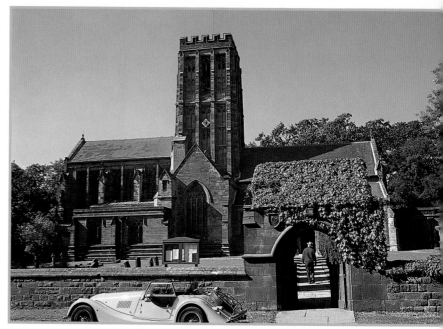

Bodley's masterpiece - Hoar Cross

One bright morning I tugged open the farmgate - sagged on its hinges since Harold went - and coasted down to Dunstall where an elegant hall overlooks a demure cricket pitch. Until quite recently the hall belonged to a man who had made his pile in cement, dredged from the gravel beds of the Trent Valley. When he died it was purchased by a man who started life as a plumber. Gravel, u-bends, anything is possible if one perseveres, if one gets that lucky break. When the hall was opened to the public on a rare occasion not so long ago, to raise funds for cancer research, all the locals poured in to sit on his gracious lawns with slabs of coffee cake, basking in his reflected glory.

Cow parsley was not yet quite in full retreat from the verges, but it was beginning to look frayed at the edges, and foxgloves and campion were starting to burst through. Cream to purple, did that not have some religious connotation? I wasn't sure. What I did know was that campion always makes me think of Margery Allingham's amateur sleuth, Albert ('A person of importance') who was forever driving round in open top sports cars, solving mysteries beyond the capacity of the police, and rescuing damsels in distress

from the clutches of smugglers and thieves. I pretty much saw myself in such a role, keeping an alert eye out on these journeys for the opportunity to do good deeds with all due modesty - even if it meant rescuing damsels who didn't necessarily want to be rescued.

Needwood Forest is rich in by-roads. This is where I learnt to drive; enjoying the countryside as much (if not more) than the motoring. We lived in a three-storey, six-bedroom Georgian house (which my parents had purchased in 1961 for £3,900) at the end of a lengthy private drive and I was able to grasp the rudiments of gear change and steering before entering upon the Queen's Highway in the company of a lugubrious instructor prone to shouting instructions at the last possible moment. I celebrated my last lesson by driving him through a set of red lights in Burton's busiest thoroughfare before taking my test and passing first time.

Scotch Hill is a local beauty spot. The road switchbacks precipitously to cross a sequence of brooks which drain into the Trent near Alrewas. My father accompanied me on those nascent drives, and on one wintry day we

The Market Cross - Abbot's Bromley

in the midlands). It is also known (in narrower and more educated circles) for the sheer size and beauty of its parish church, 'Bodley's masterpiece' according to the *Shell Guide* and 'one of the most beautiful 19th century churches in England'. I would have liked to look inside, but it was locked. It was God's day off.

I progressed, poetically to Abbot's Bromley, celebrated for its annual Horn Dance and for the girl's boarding school of St Mary & St Anne. The Horn Dance is held on the first Monday in September, and I will refrain from quoting G. K. Chesterton on the subject of Morris Dancing. A crocodile of schoolgirls of perhaps eleven summers was in the act of crossing a zebra crossing between two portions of the establishment. In blue cotton summer dresses and white ankle socks they would never look so lovely to male eyes again without invoking ambivalent passions. By Staffordshire standards, which are not notably high, Abbot's Bromley is a picturesque village. Its brick, public-house-punctuated thoroughfare opens out into a broad green dominated by a market cross.

On summer weekends, Ashmore's prize-winning ice cream vans trundle out from Uttoxeter to the banks of Blithfield Reservoir and do a roaring trade. Just as well for my waistline that this was a weekday. I roared downhill to the long causeway which cuts the six mile in circumference reservoir almost in half. It was built in 1953 by damming the River Blithe and is used by the South Staffordshire Water Company to provide drinking water to one and a half million people. Now yachtsmen and anglers enjoy good sport on its glittering waters, birdwatchers focus on their quarry through expensive binoculars and telescopes, and mere mortals such as I lick their ninety-nines and stare at our own little inland sea wondering when the tide will turn.

Breasting the rise beyond the reservoir, there lay Cannock Chase in all its glory. But first I had business to transact in what I once called in one of my canal guides, the scurrilous little town of Rugeley. A woman with a red watering can was refreshing her pot plants outside one of the old railway cottages preceding a long retaining wall made out of blue Staffordshire bricks. Under the railway and over the Trent I went on an ungainly bridge which looks as though it may once have been gas lit. We used to shop on Saturday mornings in Rugeley, but now we favour Uttoxeter, which just shows how increasingly sophisticated we have grown. I couldn't remember having to pay to park. Surreptitiously, I swapped hats, exchanging the natty little straw number I'd chosen to accompany me on these journeys for an

slithered to a halt on Scotch Hill in the snow, and only managed to progress by dint of placing the car's carpet mats under the wheels. Resourceful is my middle name. Or should that be remorseful? Fathers and sons: we say what we mean, but we sometimes lack the services of an interpreter.

At Newchurch I crossed the busy A515 and went down through the Duchy of Lancaster's woodland towards Hoar Cross. When I was ten our telephone number was Hoar Cross 241, now - even in the sticks - we need eleven numbers to identify us. I might have driven straight on past the rather cliquey Meynell Ingram Arms (where Jackie and I did some courting, too shy to speak in front of the rather posh habitués) but veered instead to the left, so as to enjoy the luxury of the ford which adorns the cover of this book. Let's just say I made a bit of a splash, and leave it at that.

Hoar Cross is famous (at least in the midlands) for its Hall which has now become a health spa frequented by people who are celebrities (at least

Man's inhumanity to man - German Cemetery, Cannock Chase

46

ubiquitous all American baseball cap much more to Rugeley's taste.

I had parked near the pet shop where we once enthusiastically purchased a black lop-eared Dutch rabbit which we called Peter. Though ostensibly Tamar's, as all parents will know, pets have a way of becoming a parental responsibility. Not that I minded, Peter and I were soul mates, sharing a similar outlook on the world's iniquities, a mutual love of Mahler, and a passion for Pontefract cakes. He would come into my office and we'd chew the cud for hours. Well, actually, he preferred to chew through my telephone wires, but I knew instinctively how he felt, and there were times when I just felt like pooing all over the carpet too.

My mission today was to try and find some film for my camera. Transparency film seems to be regarded as *passé* in some retail circles as the stocking of flannelette pyjamas, liver salts and bicycle clips. Increasingly, I cling to the old ways. I was brought up in journalism to believe that medium format transparency film gave the best results where print reproduction was concerned. I do not accept that digital photography is yet able to compete where quality, as opposed to ease, is the criteria. Hence I went hunting round Rugeley, and was pleasantly surprised when the assistant at the photographic counter in Boots was able not only to supply me with process paid transparency film, but also to inform me that it is made for Boots by Agfa, a trade secret I am happy to subscribe to. On reflection, I suppose transparency film carries with it an anorak image of serious amateurs falling upon unwitting guests and forcing them to sit through slide shows of holidays in Bridlington.

When I first knew Rugeley there was still a working coal mine on its doorstep. A spanking post war pit at that, with a workforce of exiled Scots and East European refugees, designed to provide coal on demand for the adjacent power station. Now it is 'cheaper' to rail coal in from opencast mines in Ayrshire or coal imported from Australia than coal dug in Rugeley. And if the economics of that defeat you, you are in broad company.

Of Rugeley's other delights I'll be brief, because time is of the essence. I can recommend the Market Hall, a cornucopia of butchers, milliners, and dealers in cut price greetings cards and long flat slabs of toffee for the sweet of tooth. From adjacent bus stops you can catch a Green Bus to Cannock, a memorable journey up steep hills, past post-industrial pit towns and through forest glades hiding shy deer to the accompanying hubbub of local slander and gossip. Also worthy of a mention in dispatches is George & Berties, a peculiarly continental style cafe, almost Belgian in its surrealness, where you sit on high stools round a central counter drinking weak black coffee and munching lukewarm sausage rolls. It stands on Albion Street, opposite the offices of the Hanley Economic Building Society, not one of the financial services sector's big players. We loved George & Berties when Tamar was little, and when Jackie was taken into hospital to produce Eden, the waitresses asked Tamar and I - in the hushed tones, with which women speak of the miracle of birth - if she'd 'gone in' as men might speak of a spectacular goal or a winning putt. I called in, for auld lang syne, and found it hardly changed, the coffee still not particularly acquainted with caffeine, the sausage rolls still deliciously tepid. Seemingly the topics of conversation - births, marriages, deaths and infidelity - were still legal tender. Only I was older, and balder, and fatter, and staring astigmatically down the prickley, gorsey slope to middle age.

Driving out of Rugeley I took the turn for Damascus, motoring through Coal Board housing schemes until the tired little town heaved a phlegmatic sigh and gave way to the bracken and Scots pine of The Chase. Consisting of twenty-eight square miles of wild countryside, officially designated as being of Outstanding Beauty, Cannock Chase provides a welcome escape resource for millions of West Midlanders. If you live in a tower block in Lichfield, or Stafford, or Wolverhampton or Walsall you need only amass the money for a bus ride to find solace in the neat corridors of conifer plantations, ancient woodlands or the heathery open moors of The Chase.

My mission had a more poignant edge to it. Sixty years ago in another forest, thousands of Poles were summarily and cynically shot through the head and dumped into mass graves amidst scenes of horror too appalling to contemplate. After the Second World War many Poles found a new life in Staffordshire, happy to forget the past, but not the outrageous fate of their fellow citizens. Near Broadhurst Green, high up in the lonely centre of The Chase, they erected a small memorial to the murdered of Katyn. For many years there was confusion as to who had committed the atrocity, the Nazis or the Red Army. Standing amidst birdsong and summery scents beside the monument on that June morning, it seemed to be somehow irrelevant who had been responsible for the massacre. I felt like a teacher prepared to punish the whole class in the absence of a clear culprit.

To achieve some sense of perspective I motored a mile or two to the German War Cemetery. I might equally have gone to the Commonwealth War Cemetery. Cannock Chase was considered an appropriate place in which

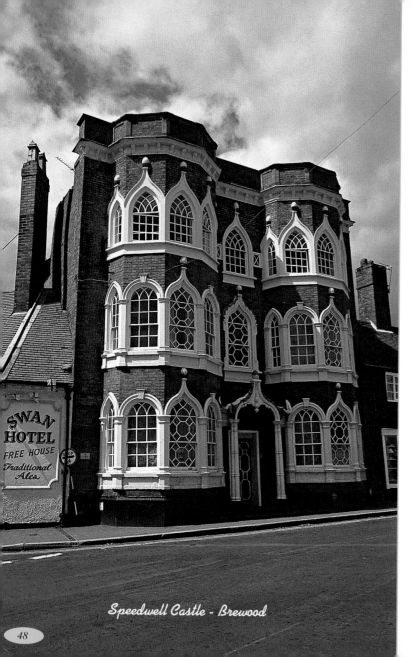

Speedwell Castle - Brewood

to lay the dead to rest as it had been such a busy military training ground during the two world wars. But somehow there is a more acute sadness in the sight of 'enemy' graves, the sheer futility of it all is even more apparent. Save for a man cutting the grass, I was the only living occupant of the cemetery. I perambulated slowly between the massed ranks of grey headstones, each bearing the names of two soldiers, as though there was comfort to be had in company, even in the earth. The sun went in and out of the clouds like mankind goes in and out of war. In the visitor's book I read that Werner Issmer of Pfozeim had been at the cemetery on the 9th of June writing: 'a beautiful resting place for my cousin, thank you'. I filled my name in and added 'Gruss Gott', which is exactly what I might have said to any of the dead had our paths crossed in some other woodland setting in time and space.

On the outskirts of Penkridge I passed over the M6, gridlocked southbound. Post-Jubilee flags were fluttering in the narrow main street, unnaturally quiet because everyone was down in the fields beside the River Penk where the town's immensely popular market was in full swing. There was chaos in the car park. People were pouring out of the market carrying little blue carrier bags containing all their newly acquired purchases. I pressed on, over the ancient packhorse bridge at Cuttlestone and through the gentle countryside of the Penk Valley to Brewood, pronounced 'Brood'. And Brewood does seem to brood, happily so, a timeless sort of place linked only to the outside world by the hourly arrival and departure of the characterful Green Bus services. When I first encountered Brewood, researching a guide book to the Shropshire Union Canal in 1981, the buses were even more archaic than now, and I have fond memory of a lovely journey along the dusty lanes to Wheaton Aston in a half-cab double-decker, my ticket being dispensed to me from a rack of many colours, and validated with a punching machine which tinged joyfully at each transaction.

By high-hedged lanes I proceeded to Boscobel where, as every schoolchild knows, King Charles II hid in an oak tree following his army's ignominious defeat at the Battle of Worcester in 1651. There were lots of schoolchildren already encamped at Boscobel when I arrived. They were being given graphic lessons in the Civil War by members of the Sealed Knot who apparently camp here annually to re-enact episodes concerning the King's flight from Worcester and subsequent escape to France. They were taking it all very seriously, a canon fired ear-shatteringly as I paid for entry, and high-pitched voices were chanting 'God Save the King' ad infinitum and with much gusto. In contrast the house itself was almost deserted. I was promised a guided tour if I assembled 'by the pump' at quarter past twelve, but

I doubted if I could afford the time, so I showed myself around (with the aid of a guide book) and enjoyed the general ambiance whilst paying scant attention to the facts: sometimes, as Sir John Squire, once a celebrated editor of *Punch*, observed, facts can be 'flies in the amber'. One slightly embarrassing fact did leap out at me from the guidebook, and that was to the effect that I had inadvertently crossed over the border into Shropshire on entering the grounds of Boscobel, but I salved my conscience with the old journalistic maxim that one should never let the facts get in the way of a good story.

I leapt quickly into the Morgan and nipped quickly back across the road into the county I was meant to be exploring. The rural corner of Staffordshire I was now traversing is really off the beaten track. Via Ivetsy Bank I made my way from Bishop's Wood to Wheaton Aston. What lyricism there is in such names, evoking images of sleepy by-ways leading you effulgently from church tower to church tower, letting you in on the best kept secrets of best kept villages. At Little Onn I pulled up to photograph the remnants of Wheaton Aston's Second World War RAF aerodrome, a tangle of overgrown Nissen huts and crumbling, grass-grown runways. For most of its short but intense history it was used in the training of aircrew, a typically monthly intake being in the region of two hundred pilots. Mostly Oxfords were employed, reaching a total of almost a hundred and fifty aircraft in 1944. After the war Polish exiles and their families were billeted here before they could be re-housed in Stafford. Aneurin Bevan landed here on October 25th 1946, having flown from Croydon on his way to a meeting in Stoke-on-Trent. I always find old aerodromes fascinating in a moving sort of way and this was no exception. War, and the great expendable pity of it all, seemed to be the underlying theme of this particular journey, I reflected, as I walked back to the car.

I challenge you to find your way from Wheaton Aston to High Offley without taking a wrong turn. Luckily the Morgan was fitted with a sophisticated route-finding mechanism. In other words I followed my nose - from pig farm to pig farm. Beyond Gnosall (drop the G and make the S sound like a Z!) the by-road I was on suddenly veered sharp left and plunged through a natural tunnel of trees into a man-made tunnel under the Birmingham & Liverpool Junction Canal. This was Thomas Telford's great Shelmore Bank, six years in the making, and only necessary at all because the local landowner didn't want his pheasants disturbed. At the far end of the embankment the

Wartime aerodrome - High Onn

road ducks under it again and comes to the little canal community of Norbury Junction. Regretably, 'junction' is a misnomer since the old canal to Shrewsbury was abandoned in 1944, but Norbury now enjoys the fruits of the leisure-orientated revival in canal boating, and is busy with holiday narrowboats all summer long, many of their crews hopefully employing the guidebooks I have been writing (and re-writing) for the last twenty years. The Junction Inn is a former (though much rebuilt) boatman's pub, and duly popular, but I fancied a pint in a more authentic setting, so I carried on northwards heading for High Offley by way of Grubb Street, where the canal negotiates a deep, lengthy, heavily wooded and reputedly haunted cutting, much of the spoil from which went into the building of Shelmore Bank. My goal was the Anchor Inn, a wonderful throwback to a simpler age. When I first began writing about canals in the Seventies there was a handful of such premises dotted about the canal system, untouched by time and the crass, uncultured marketing departments of brewers who should have known better.

Shelmore Bank, Norbury

Usually they were in the hands of elderly ladies who clung reassuringly to the old ways as folk cling to a life raft when the ship is sinking. My analogy is non-refundable. One by one I've watched them disappear as their owners have gone to join that great Licensed Victuallers Association in the sky. One by one they have either been converted into bijou dwellings, or been eagerly snapped up by this or that pub chain, and come out the other side with wacky warehouse adjuncts and food counters where your orders are processed by the pressing of a computer button: "If you'd just like to leave your credit card with me sir, in case you try to leave without paying when you feel like throwing up the contents of our delicious home-cooked menu all over the car park."

The Anchor stands shyly back from the canal, hovering behind its well-trimmed hawthorn hedge like a recluse nervously waiting to be introduced to a passing dignitary. A group of real ale aficionados - Brummies with big bellies and loud laughs - were in the garden, reverentially savouring their beer. Seeking peace and quiet I went into the bar where the landlady poured my pint of Wadworth 6X from a jug and offered to make me a cheese sandwich. I sat on a high backed bench and listened to the clicking of a grandfather clock - not so much a chronometer, more a metronome, beating out the slow rhythm which resonates throughout The Anchor like a ley line.

And when it came that cheese sandwich was just that, a cheese sandwich, beautifully unembellished, lying succinctly on a patterned tea plate as if it was 1953 and horse-drawn Thomas Claytons were still gliding by on the canal, carrying oil from Ellesmere Port to Oldbury. As if to enhance this illusion, I was joined by an elderly countryman who'd been tilling the pub's vegetable patch when I arrived. We greeted each other tentatively.

"How do?" he said.

"Hallo," I said, "Are you alright?"

"I keep doing a bit and missing a bit," he replied enigmatically. And then the landlady began to speak of a throbbing tooth.

"I'll tak em out for ee," said the countryman, with a wink in my direction. One of the Brummies came in for some pork scratchings - as they do - and the landlady's attention wavered.

"You'm a photographer?" the countryman asked pointedly.

"What gives you that impression," I laughed.

"I saw ee taking pictures on the bridge."

It occurred to me that a bright yellow Morgan might not be the best vehicle

The Anchor at High Offley

for a self-effacing writer of a retiring disposition to operate from.

"I'm driving around, writing a book," I confessed sheepishly. Normally I like to give people the impression that I'm with the Inland Revenue, it deters conversation.

"That's a nice job," he retorted enthusiastically: "I worked on the cut."

"As a boatman?" I asked, beginning to be intrigued.

"A lengthsman", he corrected me, "I worked in Betton Wood, and Grub Street and Tyrley. Seventeen miles I had at one time, and I did the locks at Tyrley and Audlem."

"Were there still working boats?" I asked.

"Nah, they'd gorn; but there wus maint'nance boats. I worked on them. Do you know the canal?"

"A bit," I lied.

"Terrible wet, sum o' them rockin's"

"I suppose they cut through the water table," I said introducing a degree of science into the conversation.

"That'll be it," he agreed: "Seven men they had in Tyrley one time, just keepin it dry."

Of such encounters is travel writing made. Usually we hacks have to make them up because nobody ever bothers to talk to us. In retrospect I may have dozed off over my Wadworth 6X and dreamed the countryman up. I'll leave that to your intuition as we progress along the next leg of our Staffordshire journey in an easterly direction, Eccleshall bound. I met nothing on the road but a milk tanker. For once I was glad to be fifty and old enough to remember churns awaiting collection at the end of the drive, or partially immersed in becks and brooks and burns to keep cool. Eccleshall appeared like a metropolis in the context of the backwoods I'd been savouring. A handsome main street is enhanced by an eclectic melange of architectural periods and styles; one or two of the upper storeys being picturesquely supported on arches.

I crossed the River Sow and went through Chebsey, coming upon a 'road liable to flooding' sign as one might talk of someone being 'prone to bouts of anxiety'. It brought to mind a line in my final school report, whereby, in the teacher's opinion I 'worried more about the future than I appeared to'. He did me more credit than I necessarily deserved, somehow implying that the fate of mankind rested uneasily upon my eighteen year old shoulders, but that he thought that, in the long run and on balance, I'd be up to the job of saving civilization single-handedly. Only in hindsight have I understood how perceptive he was.

Similar responsibility was thrust upon me as soon as I ducked down to enter Izaak Walton's Cottage at Shallowford.

"Are you local?" twittered the two ladies behind the counter. "We need everyone to sign our petition. They want to close us down to save money. You're, not local? Even better!"

'They', of course, were the local authority, who hitherto had supported this charming little piscatorial shrine, but now the accountants had their knives out, looking for easy victims of a cost-cutting regime. Not wishing to disappoint the ladies, I signed the petition as Count Zenilinsky of Zagreb, adding in the comments column, that in my country petty officials seen to be swimming against the will of the people, are quietly taken from their homes in the depths of night, garrotted and left in shallow graves in the forest, all trace of their previous existence expunged from all records.

Impressed by my credentials, the ladies led me to the first floor, plied me with tea and biscuits and left me to watch a video concerning the lore

of fishing in general and Izaak Walton in particular. My father was a keen fisherman, as subsequent chapters will reveal, and so the nuances of angling are not entirely lost on me. In an adjoining room, display cases contained fishing rods of greenheart, cane and bamboo, 'Small Nottinghams' and 'Large Birminghams', bait kettles and fly tins, reels from Malloch's, Hardy's and Embro's. Above the stairs hung glass cases of stuffed fish: bream, salmon, perch, and a pike caught in Gailey Top Pool by a delighted Mr Meakin in 1906. If only all our achievements were so preserved for posterity, we would all be immortal.

Izaak Walton was embroiled in the Civil War, so there was another connecting thread in my day. A staunch Royalist, he fled the City of London and moved all the way to Clerkenwell. Much of *The Compleat Angler* concerns his fishing activities on the rivers Ware and Lee in Hertfordshire. The book's survival as a small classic is a small miracle of irrelevance. Were I to write a small monograph entitled *The Compleat Trainspotter*, what chance would I have of it being still 'in print' four hundred years from now, let alone next month.

Walton purchased the cottage at Shallowford, together with the adjoining farm in 1655. In his will he altruistically bequeathed it to the town of Stafford, its annual rental to be used for charitable purposes, such as the purchase of coal for poor people. Those employees of the local authority who would shut it down, might do well to consider the spirit of Walton's will. The cottage opened as a museum as long ago as 1924. Passing steam locomotives on the adjacent LMS main line set its thatched roof on fire in 1927 and 1938.

I went out into the herb garden at the rear of the cottage. Fortunately I had a tape measure with me and was able to authenticate the measurements quoted in a leaflet acquired within the museum. 'The herb garden is 50ft by 35ft (15m by 10.6m) and is divided into two large and two small beds. The beds are separated by wide grass paths and the garden is surrounded on two sides by Yew hedges'. Irrespective of their impressive aggregate volume, the herbs were aromatically

"'Small Nottinghams' and 'Large Birminghams', bait kettles and fly tins, reels from Malloch's, Hardy's and Embro's."

Izaak Walton's Cottage, Shallowford

enjoyable too. Examples were for sale and I purchased a gold lemon balm as a souvenir of my visit much as other folk acquire stickers with which to fill the back windows of their cars: Bude, Ilfracombe, Weston-super-Mare, Barry Island, Barmouth, Toyota.

I bid farewell to the ladies. They urged me to call again if I was ever in the neighbourhood. I promised them faithfully to do so, but told them to be brave and bear in mind that I was on the run from counter-revolutionaries and insurgents, evil men who would shut down all the fishing museums east of the Adriatic if they had their nefarious way.

Norton Bridge is the railway age equivalent of Norbury Junction, though here both the original Grand Junction and North Staffordshire routes remain very much in use and virtually monopolised by Richard Branson's Virgin Trains: their futuristic, aerodynamic shapes anachronistically at odds with the coterie of Victorian railwaymen's cottages which overlook the isolated station. I reached Stone at 3.45pm. Stone is a nice small town,

Flint mill interior - the grinding pan

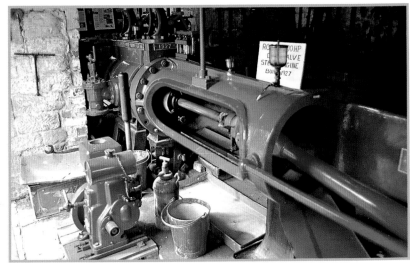

Flint mill interior - the Robey engine

much infatuated with the Trent & Mersey Canal which slopes through it. It was formerly the home of Joules and Bents breweries. As late as the 1950s, Joules' telephone number was Stone 1. In 1970 they were taken over by Bass Charrington and Stalinised out of existence. Stone railway station masquerades as a Jacobean mansion. No longer staffed by rail employees (they work in call centres now) there are hopes that it may become a community centre.

The A520 from Stone to Leek is a main road not entirely devoid of character, but when viewed from behind a slow moving lorry bearing galvanized farm gates, much of its appeal remains hidden - literally! I reached Cheddleton at 4.20pm. There are three interesting things to see in Cheddleton, but two of them were closed. St Edward's Church contains some fine Pre-Raphaelite stained glass, the work of William Morris: the caretaker locks up at 4pm - on the dot. The railway station has been preserved by the Churnet Valley Railway who operate steam trains along that eponymously secluded valley most *weekends*. That left me with the Cheddleton Flint Mill Museum, and for once in my life it did not represent the short straw. To call the Flint Mill a *museum* would be to do it a disservice. It is a museum in the sense that it houses a collection of objects of historical

significance, yet it exhibits these in such a naturally informal and appropriate manner as to suspend any sense that what you are seeing is *preserved*, as opposed to functioning *commercially*. This feeling is further enhanced by the apparent lack of curatorial staff. In the whole half hour or so that I was there (and I wished I'd had much longer - not to see more, but to simply soak up the atmosphere) I encountered no other living being. Solely the machinery was alive, a sibilant system of cogwheels and belts powered with a gently revolving waterwheel driven by the waters of the River Churnet, and there is no more soothing a sound than the turning and dripping of a waterwheel.

There has been a mill in Cheddleton since medieval times. In 1580 there were 'two mills under one roof': one a corn mill the other used for the washing of woollen cloth. The grinding of flint did not begin until the 1770s, by which time the Caldon Canal had been constructed past the door. Flint is a very durable mineral which is used to add strength to pottery. Many mills in North Staffordshire were converted into flint mills at the end of the 18th century to see to the voracious needs of The Potteries, for it could be a far more lucrative trade than agricultural milling. A factor in Cheddleton Flint Mill's success was its proximity to the canal, and a typical example of the kind of craft used to bring flint to the mill is permanently moored nearby.

Vienna was built by the famous canal carrying firm of Fellow, Morton & Clayton. Seventy-two feet in length by seven in beam, *Vienna* was a 'butty' boat built in Saltley, Birmingham in 1911 at an estimated cost of £200. In its working days it would have been more familiar with the Grand Union Canal between London and Birmingham, but it was rescued by the Flint Mill Industrial Heritage Trust in 1974 and restored for display at Cheddleton at a cost of £3,500. In 1999 the boat was rebuilt with a steel bottom in place of the original of elm to ensure its long term survival. Various bodies sponsored this work to the tune of £36,000! Preservation is an increasingly expensive business.

Leek is my sort of town - remote, aloof, a throwback, and inclined to melancholic fits of self-doubt - I fit the description perfectly. It has cobbled streets, a church by Norman Shaw, and a lot of positively Ruritanian Victorian architecture by a local man - with the good old northern name of Sugden - who had a penchant for leonine ornamentation. There's an indoor buttermarket (which sells, amongst other things, real farm-packed butter), a fabulous tearoom called Greystones - so good that you invariably have to queue to get in - and a well-stocked secondhand bookshop. It is also the location of Asplin's Oatcake Shop. Oatcakes are a North Staffordshire delicacy that have so far resisted all attempts to popularise them further afield. As a means of wrapping other foods it rivals the French crepe, Indian chapatti and Mexican taco, but apart from some half-hearted supermarket retailing, it has barely travelled beyond Biddulph. Yet there are fifty to sixty oatcake retailers in and around Stoke-on-Trent and the integrity of each maker's recipe is sacrosanct. Lindsay Asplin locks himself in his 'preparation room' in the watches of the night to 'fill the jowel' with his own top secret mixture, before emerging to pass it on to his assistants who will spread it on the griddle.

"I'm legally prevented from divulging the recipe to a third party," he told me. "I bought the recipe from my aunty and she bought it from my grandparents. People occasionally come in and say they're leaving the area, and that they won't be able to cope without Asplins' Oatcakes, and could I quietly let them have the recipe. But I can't trust anyone. They might be spying for another oatcake maker!"

I could see from Lindsay's expression just how serious, the cloak & dagger, cut-throat world of the oatcake industry is, and how rivals might stoop to who knows what level of skullduggery to uncover the ingredients of another recipe. Lindsay thinks that the hitherto parochial oatcake only needs money and marketing muscle thrown at it and, hey presto, there'll be oatcake drive-thrus on the edge of every town nationwide. Perhaps he's got a point, but little old reactionary me can't help feeling that the wider availability of regional dishes somehow negates their inherent appeal.

The A53 runs in a north-easterly direction out of Leek on its last lap to Buxton, carrying motorists into a wild moorland landscape cheek by jowl with the Cheshire border. These are not really the Midlands any more I thought, this is The North! I might have been some wild-west bandit with a price on my head, banned from crossing the county line. So I stopped short of it, turning off to my left just after Upper Hulme and parking by the side of the road to climb to the top of Ramshaw Rocks. I chose the fiendishly difficult South Col approach. All the authoritative mountaineering manuals counsel against it, but the library had written me, what I considered an unnecessarily terse letter, demanding them back. Neither had I prepared for the ascent by bringing any equipment with me. I had only a Union Jack, a large bar of Kendal Mint Cake, and a Potteries Motor Traction timetable.

I am far too tactful to alarm you with graphic details of my climb. On the way I came upon the remains of unfortunates who had perished in the attempt to reach the top. One man had a hideously fixed grin on his face with which to meet his maker, as if he'd been forced to watch reruns of Pop Idol before setting out. Others had scrawled poignant messages to their kith and kin: 'Mother, I'll be a bit late for tea'; 'Vera, I cashed the endowment in to fuel my pigeon racing neurosis; 'Jane, I have another wife and six children in Macclesfield, if I survive I can explain everything'.

The climb seemed to take an eternity, but when I looked at my watch as I sought the last few footholds from which to hoist myself on to the top, only eight minutes seemed to have elapsed; a phenomenon of the volcanic properties present in the rock perhaps. Heaving myself on to the summit with a sigh of relief not unmingled with pride, I heard a small voice behind me. It appeared to come from a six year old girl who was standing beside a large red setter.

"Don't worry about the dog, mister," she said soothingly, "Ma says 'is bite's always worse than 'is bark! I watched you coming up the long way round. That's a nice hat you're wearing ..."

Morgan & mountaineer - Ramshaw Rocks

Wayside Shrine, the Goyt Valley

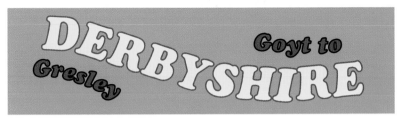

Goyt to DERBYSHIRE
Gresley

On the high moors which separate Buxton from Whaley Bridge, a by-road corkscrews down from the A5002 to the reservoir-filled base of the Goyt Valley. I parked by a wayside Catholic shrine to Our Lady and heaved myself out of the Morgan to stretch my legs. Larks were singing somewhere invisibly above me and, down in the valley - where an old green road runs more directly, but also more precipitously, than the present main road - a curlew was calling. Going for a day out in Derbyshire for me is like being invited to a party - I do not expect to enjoy it very much, but sometimes I can be pleasantly surprised.

The Goyt Valley's gleaming reservoirs, Errwood and Fernilee supply water to the kitchen sinks of Stockport. They also provide solace to the benighted inhabitants of that town. On this bright morning the car park was filled with them. Early retired in Marks & Spencer pullovers selected by their wives. Bald or grey but good for a few years yet. Lost only for a purpose in life and looking up from the *Daily Mail* to see if the water can provide inspiration. Instead they see a fellow traveller zooming by in a cloud of dust and a yellow sports car, and they wonder where they've gone wrong, and why fortune hasn't smiled so benevolently upon them. How could they know that the man in the Morgan has his own monsters to slay? He's on the run from the ample bosom of Middle Age, and if he could, he would go on driving for ever, for travel is the ultimate escape.

If he could drive rapidly enough, faster than the speed of light for instance, he would use the Morgan as a time machine, and find his way back to 1972, when he first familiarised himself with this back-road through the Goyt Valley, as a section of the route he devised to get him to and from Manchester Polytechnic without touching a main road. In those days the road was open in either direction. Now, to cater for the day-trippers, it is 'traffic-managed' into one way. Then, on dripping November evenings, it reminded him of roads corkscrewing down from alpine passes, now it looked

Cotton grass - Axe Edge Moor

to him like the sea-front at Mablethorpe. Yet the rhododendrons were still ablaze, planted for an inconceivable posterity by the Grimshawes of Errwood Hall, demolished in the 1930s as Fernilee Reservoir was being constructed. The driver of the sports car parked briefly on double yellow lines so as to photograph them embellishing a backwater, and wished he was twenty again and capable of foresight.

Derbyshire is a long, narrow county. It hardly seems plausible that Glossop and Swadlincote can be spoken of in the same breath. The morass of Kinder Scout seems little related to the post-industrial mining scars of Woodville. And yet counties are like families. They are thrown together genetically, and likenesses are often arbitrary. The ritual of driving home for the weekend (for he was not over-enamoured with the more depraved aspects of what passed for a student's social life, my twenty year old self) illustrated just how different one end of a county can be from another. Shaking free from Stockport's urban tentacles, he would turn right off the A6 at Disley and never see an A road again until the outskirts of Ashbourne reached out to embrace him. Over the shoulder of Whaley Moor he entered Derbyshire and would stay therein until he crossed the River Dove at Sudbury. He would be anticipating steak & kidney pie for tea and wondering if Derby

County would win at the Baseball Ground the following afternoon.

I caught up with a cyclist as the road left the shelter of the woods and climbed on to a moorland plateau. He was wearing a colourful Spanish cycling shirt. Sometimes I think the attraction of cycling for these blokes is not so much the open road but the chance to adorn themselves in bright colours they wouldn't be seen dead in in the day job. The road zig-zagged across a chuckling stream, a childlike watercourse, the headwaters of the Goyt itself, destined to go into partnership with the Tame at Stockport and call themselves the Mersey. 'Flow on little river,' I called back through my slipstream, 'if you knew what awaits you, you'd want to flow uphill, like the rest of us!'

Dodging sheep on the road, I drove the Morgan up on to Axe Edge Moor where cotton grass billowed under high skies. Navigating from memory, I crossed the A54 and the A53. The road took on a sinister aspect as it skirted the quarry workings of Harpur Hill. Security fencing guarded enigmatic underground installations and, at a lay-by, a Derbyshire Constabulary notice appealed for information concerning the discovery of the body of a white male in a burnt out car at this location the month before. I shuddered, and pressed on, with one eye over my shoulder, hurtling down the next hill at 38 mph.

Washing hung voluminously from the line at Harley Grange, and I came down with a bump into a more ordered and seemly world delineated by limestone walls. Cows chewed comfortingly in pastures and it was silage time. I crossed the B5053 and drove through Earl Sterndale, noting a pub called The Quiet Woman, quiet, according to the pub sign, solely because she had been beheaded! An odd story concerns the church which was hit by an incendiary bomb on the night of the 9th of January 1941 and completely gutted. A wedding was held in the ruins the day after.

I had forgotten the conical hill which confronts you as you drive southwards out of the village. Going over a once familiar road is like playing a long forgotten song. Shapes and phrases come back to you, as do associations. Suddenly I was twenty-two again and in love. Anything seemed possible. There was no such thing as an horizon; optimism, a heady and virtuous drug, exploded in my veins.

I enjoyed the three years I spent in Manchester immensely. After a frustrating year at art school, the certainties of a polytechnic and a course in print technology were reassuring. Sometimes it doesn't matter what you do so long as what you do has a shape and definition to it. Manchester meant security and a sense of belonging. The complexities of print were not taxing. I trod water effectively in all subjects save science, in which, I proudly achieved only 6%. The subject so numbed me, that on one occasion I fell cacophonously from a high laboratory stool in the middle of a lecture; later inventing a pen & paper based football game with which to while away the unintelligible hours. Science! They might just as well have tried to teach me Serbo-Croat. It meant nothing. It would have been my nadir were it not for Work Study, a series of exercises in time and motion which climaxed in a visit to a steam laundry. We were required to write an essay summarising our reaction. I submitted a play in which the hero was so disorientated by the demands of his betters that he went berserk. The lecturer, a young Jewish woman, never acknowledged my presence thereafter. The mistrust was mutual. I have never had time for anyone who didn't make something in the broadest sense. The world is too full of organisers who live off the efforts of others like eunuchs in a harem.

In the Seventies I would place my Mini into neutral and coast through the sinuous curves of Long Dale. The Morgan similarly obliged. Only the swish of tyres intruded on lark song above. I leaned back in the driving seat and looked up at the high clouds in the blue sky. In neighbouring fields, corrugated lines of cut grass had been whisked up into rows to dry. By Custard Field Farm I entered Long Dale. Steep sided, rocky and rippled, it always made me think of the Crimea, Tennyson and the *Charge of the Light Brigade*:

> Their's not to reason why,
> Their's but to do and die.

Up on the ridge, silhouetted against the horizon, a French General watched the yellow Morgan hurtle down the valley of death, turned to a colleague and remarked: "C'est magnifique, mais ce n'est pas La Gare."

I was peckish and thirsty and thought I might be able to find refreshments in Hartington. Technically, this was true, but in order to do so I would have had to fight my way through a scrum of tour coach parties and elderly couples hovering over souvenirs. So I didn't even attempt to park, but pressed on along the gated road to Pilsbury. It was a delicious road and I could tell that even the Morgan was happy to be ambling along its pot-holed

Dovedale - Pilsbury

surface. The delightful aroma of hot engine oil wafted up from the long yellow bonnet and mingled with the musky smell of waving cow parsley. The walnut dashboard gleamed like alabaster. Down to my left I caught glimpses of the Dove and thought of Izaak Walton and the little fishing museum in his old home at Shallowford. Gates came at frequent intervals and reminded me of locks on a canal, welcome opportunities for exercise. The first two I did myself, the third was opened for me by a hiking gentleman of clerical bent.

"I suppose you want me to tip you a penny for that," I joked.

"On no," he chuckled ecclesiastically, adding "it would be much more than that!" as if he had a leaking 15th century church roof to maintain and devoutly believed that I had been miraculously sent down from Heaven in a fast sports car with offers of unlimited largesse.

Broadmeadow Hall stood out across the valley - serene and snug, mullioned and mellow - only it was in Staffordshire, and I had no business taking notice of it. In any case, at Pilsbury the road gets fed up of wandering along the valley floor and strikes westwards, climbing abruptly back into the hills like a serious hiker. A mile further on I rejoined the road I had journeyed down barely half an hour before, but on this occasion I turned left at Custard Field

Farm, taking the road to Parlsey Hay. In my Manchester days the old railway earthworks in the vicinity of Parsley Hay were comparatively recently abandoned. It seemed plausible that ghost trains might still negotiate them in the middle of scented summer nights. Now, however, they are hugely popular routes for ramblers, riders and cyclists. This may fill purists with regret, but one wishes that all lost railways might have been converted into public rights of way instead of being broken up piecemeal and sold or stolen by landowners, farmers and industrialists.

Much as I mourned the loss of the railway, the sign of a cafe by the bicycle hire centre was most welcome, for the hour of noon had passed and sustenance was required if my sugar levels were not to drop dangerously low. I was served by a man who looked as if he was more used to making boiler stays than ham and cheese sandwiches. I was grateful that his hands were clad in disposable gloves, fearing otherwise that the choice of fillings might be limited to oil, turpentine and Swarfega. Munching away, I strolled along the High Peak Trail pretending to be the 10.15 from Uttoxeter to Buxton, inexplicably running late, for according to the 1951 timetable on my shelves at home I should have called at Parsley Hay at 11.31. Perhaps there had been cows on the line at Norbury & Ellastone or Clifton for Mayfield or Thorpe Cloud (for Dovedale), perhaps some poetically minded passenger had pulled the communication cord so as to enable him to complete the sonnet he had been inspired to write by the ravishing landscape panoramically presented through the compartment window. Then four young women hoved into view, totally destroying my daydream, though it is not often one can feel chagrin at such a sight.

Tick tock, tick tock goes time, and we flatter ourselves that we keep pace with it. But when we turn and look back, it transpires that we have come no distance at all. A quarter of a century had ricocheted by since I last stood in the stone circle at Arbor Low. These stones are Derbyshire's Avebury, its Rollright, its Stonehenge, but because they are recumbent they have not attained popularity with the general public, neither have they been 'marketed' by the tourist board, so they sit in their hollowed cup of a hillside, impervious to the passage of time, and if I go and visit them every twenty-five years or so, it will be me that changes, not them. One more visit, perhaps, and then I will be too infirm to walk up the hill. When I came here with Alison Foster, in 1974, on one of our sporadic walks across the limestone table-

land, I was learning to be a printer. Now what was I learning? That time is a traitor.

A sign pointed through the farmyard 'to the circle' as if I was about to take my place in a theatre or auditorium. In a neighbouring field the farmer was cutting hay. Judging by the plethora of sticky and aromatic cow pats, the stones had just recently been vacated by a herd of cattle. Four thousand years old, the forty-six stones lay enigmatically pointing inwards towards the central sanctuary. Even experts can only guess as to their significance. In another four thousand years will it be as difficult to define the purpose of Pride Park, or is that already impossible?

I walked slowly around the lip of the circle, widening my focus from time to time out towards an infinity of limestone walled countryside, dappled under cotton wool clouds into areas of shadow and light, almost blanched where the fields had already been cut. As I came back down from the circle the tractor had stopped cutting and I could see that the farmer's wife had brought out his lunch. A tiny boy accompanied her to see his dad. It was a ritual as ancient as the stones. They watched me approach the stile with the shyness of sheepdogs.

"A good dry day for cutting," I called, and with that they thawed and smiled and laughed back:

"'Bout time too!"

Back at the car park a family had just drawn up. Husband and wife were reading the interpretive board, but he was not easily impressed.

"Bit more to it than that," he told her, shaking his dubious thickset head, "pure conjecture that, pure conjecture ..."

I drove through a Youlgreave nodding post-prandially. An old man was taking his ease outside the Bull's Head. A boy, who would have been a boy when he was a boy, came out of the butchers with some chops for his lonely tea. I passed a very pleasant looking cricket ground at the eastern end of the village. A Hulleys of Baslow bus came by me and then the River Lathkill (one of Alison's favourites) joined me for a mile or two before I turned on to the B5056, making for Winster. The B5056 is a lovely little road linking Ashbourne with Bakewell, and it is one we have come to know quite well in recent years on trips to watch Eden play football for Smallwood Manor against St Anselms; rollicking affairs with no quarter given, at least amongst the parents.

Arbor Low

Winster was as comatose as Youlgreave. The handsome Market House dates from the late 17th century and belongs now to the National Trust who use it as an information centre. I found a propitiously close parking slot and went inside. No one was there, but the walls contained some interesting display panels, giving considerable coverage to the Winster Morris Dancers who enjoy close links with the Sbandieratori of San Benedetto in Italy. Winster's Morris Men were originally mostly lead miners and Cecil Sharp came to listen to their folksongs, meeting them as they came off shift at the Mill Close Mine in 1908.

I will paint in my passage through Matlock Bath with swift brushstrokes. Its excesses, its worldly temptations of the flesh (which, judging by the ill-concealed rolls of fat adorning many passers-by, are difficult to resist) belong in a different sort of book altogether, though if I had had more time I might have been tempted to take a bag of fish & chips myself and row a hired boat up into shady corner of the Derwent. Driving swiftly past the parked up lines of motorcyclists, looking excruciatingly hot in their leathers, some lines of Betjeman came into my head:

> *From Matlock Bath's half-timbered station*
> *I see the black dissenting spire -*

And there, out of the corner of my traffic conscious eye, was indeed a church spire of some presence, so I began to feel as if I was driving through the delightful old rascal's poem, and would have enjoyed his chuckling presence in the passenger seat, were such a deal been capable of being struck with the authorities in the next life. An enduring image of Sir John, wheelchair-bound and wracked with Parkinson's came to mind as, in one of his last broadcast interviews, he is asked had he had any regrets:

"I would have liked more sex," he admits with a wry giggle. Obviously he had never been driven around in a Morgan.

Turning off the A6 at Cromford, I decided to spend a precious half an hour in Scarthin Books. It proved a shrewd decision, because I came back out with two *Shell Guides* tucked under my arm - *Derbyshire* and *Oxfordshire* - the former very handy and topical in the circumstances, the latter an early John Piper edition of considerable worth and charm. What great books these

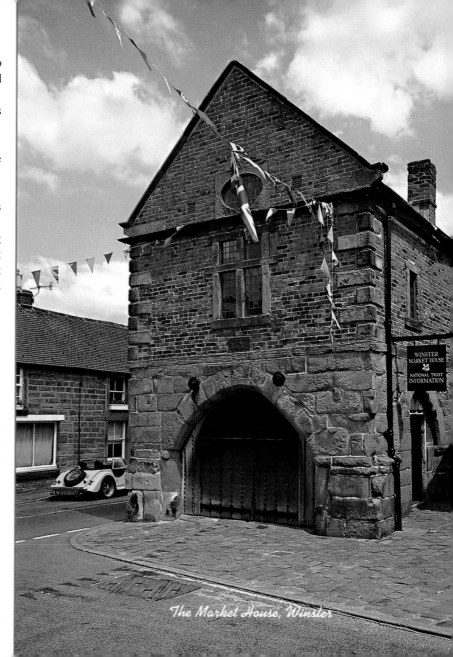

The Market House, Winster

were, and how much one wishes that some equivalent were readily available today. Perhaps the absence of such a well written and photographed series of topographical guide books hints at a deeper malaise, a lack of public interest in Britain's geography. Never before has the landscape been so accessible to all and sundry, and now never before have we been so disinterested in its fabric. Possibly this is because we have become lazy. The great tourist boom does it all for us now. We don't need to think for ourselves: leaflets pre-select our itineraries, visitor centres chaperone our response.

My Uncle Wilf would have shuddered in disgust. He was an inveterate traveller of England's by-roads. From their home in York, he and Auntie Olive would depart on great all-encompassing circles of exploration, eschewing the shortest distance between two places as lacking in imagination. Churches, mills, battlefields, railway stations, such were the nodal points of their journeys. Taking me back to York one day for a holiday, my ten year old self was much taken with a route that took in Ashbourne, Matlock, Chesterfield, Doncaster, Goole and Selby in preference to my father's break-neck adherence to the A1. A history master at Archbishop Holgate's Grammar School, one evening he drove me out to Marston Moor and lucidly explained the disposition of the waring factions. He had a great sense of humour and a great love of classical music. On his gramophone on Sunday afternoons following Olive's roast beef and Yorkshire Pudding repasts, I first heard Shostakovich's *Second Piano Concerto* and Ravel's *Piano Concerto in G* on a disc played by Bernstein. Parkinson's Disease did for him, just as it did for Betjeman. Towards the end I had introduced him to Vaughan Williams's *An Oxford Elegy*. I like to think his obvious enjoyment and appreciation of it helped him into the next world. 'Why faintest thou, I wandered 'til I died' are words enough to give anyone confidence in the longest journey, and seemed appropriate for a man who had done more than his fair share of enjoyable wandering.

Wilf would have hugely enjoyed my next port of call, the Tramway

Museum at Crich, though, like me, he would have perceived irony in the salvation of an essentially urban vehicle taking place in the environs of a Derbyshire quarry. But I don't suppose the brave stalwarts who set the ball rolling in the late 1950s ever dreamt of how successful they would become, let alone that trams would make a return to English cities as indeed they have done in Manchester, Sheffield, and Birmingham, cities soon to be joined by the likes of Nottingham and Leeds. So the importance of Crich does not now lie so much in the preservation of a transport mode as in the preservation of an epoch of street life.

At the entrance to the museum a notice board welcomed the day's visiting groups - schoolchildren from Chernobyl and widows from Uttoxeter, the juxtaposition almost made me titter. The young woman behind the counter broke off from conversation with a colleague saying: "I'll just serve this lad." I looked behind me, just to make sure, but there seemed no doubt that she was referring to me. The transaction complete, I sailed out through the turnstile on a flying carpet of egotistical air, thirty years chopped off my age.

My entry pass entitled me to as much tram travel as I had an appetite for. To make matters more realistic you are given an old fashioned, pre-decimal penny to give to the conductor in exchange for a coloured ticket from the rack which hangs over his shoulder. I strolled down to the tram stop and caught the first tram down to Town End. It was a Blackpool tram dating from the 1920s. I climbed up on to the top deck as it rattled down to Town End. The museum may have started life in a bare quarry setting, but at the terminus they have painstakingly recreated the atmosphere of a small Edwardian town by simply re-erecting old, unwanted buildings, such as the Derby Assembly Rooms, on site. And all very effective it is too. It occurred to me that the Morgan would not have looked out of place rubbing shoulders with the elderly trams, and it seemed a shame to have had to have left it in the car park with all those characterless Toyotas and Hondas. Rather than change trams so early into my visit, I stayed firmly put, only swapping seats in the briefly empty tram, so as to obtain a grandstand view from what would be the front of the vehicle

> "Churches, mills, *battlefields,* railway stations, such were the *nodal points* of their journeys."

when it departed for the full run of about a mile up to the lofty terminus called the Glory Mine.

I must confess to being old enough to remember riding on Glasgow's tram system in and around Paisley. I can also remember seeing them in Sheffield. More vividly I can recall the trolleybus systems of South Shields, Newcastle, Nottingham, Derby and Bradford, and bitterly regret their demise. How can clean, swift and environmentally kind transport systems have been abandoned in favour of smog-inducing internal combustion replacements? I'm afraid the answer is easy and repetitive, the British have no talent for transport strategy.

Presently a bamboo cane poked its head over the edge of the open balcony on which I was seated. Fortunately its appearance did not herald a blow-pipe attack by a lost tribe of Peruvian pigmies, rather it was the conductor transferring the trolley pole from one end to the other. A few fellow travellers joined me on the top deck. The bell tinkled and we moved smoothly off, the tram humming purposefully along its rails, drawing power from the overhead catenary and drawing admiration from ice-cream licking crowds on the pavement below. 'This is the way to travel' I thought contentedly, remembering how the romance of a tramcar had been successfully captured by J. B. Priestley in *The Good Companions* as Inigo Jollifant and Susie Dean found love at the terminus. I suppose love can still make an entrance on the top deck of an Arriva or Stagecoach No.10 in any given British town or city you care to mention, but I can't help feeling that the soul of urban transport fluttered up to heaven when the last Glasgow tram and the last Bradford trolleybus had their power extinguished for the final time.

A welcome breeze danced about the ornate ironwork of the tram's balcony. We trundled past the pub and the ice cream parlour, the tea rooms and the tramway depot, under a hefty bridge and past a bandstand which lacked only a brass band playing extracts from *La Boheme* to make everything perfect. All the other passengers were smiling, enjoying the tram's ability to function as a time machine. We are a simple species: give us a tramcar and an ice cream cornet and a sunny afternoon and we will grin like baboons and wave to total strangers as if war and poverty and death and taxes had never been invented.

Through woods we came to the loop at Wakebridge, where a Sheffield tram was waiting patiently to pass us. The drivers exchanged a token, then we were off again, speeding - and I use the term comparatively - past a dusty quarry and on into a shady wood before emerging high on to a ledge above the Derwent Valley, drawing to a halt at the sort of rural terminus that might have been found on the outskirts of a city before speculative builders ignited the burgeoning of the suburbs and housing spread as uncontrollably as a forest fire. On the way back I alighted at Wakebridge and was glad I did, because the next downbound tram was none other than Paisley & District's No.68, an open top double-decker dating from 1919. It was nice to think that my father, born the year after it had been built, might have ridden on it from Causeyside to Rouken Glen or some such treat. Suddenly he was beside me, child being father of the man, an eager sprat of a boy anticipating ice cream and a brief escape from the shadows of a childhood which, he has hinted, though never detailed, was not always idyllic. We rode back down together. I said he could have a lift in my yellow sports car. He thought I was teasing, gave me a huge grin and disappeared into the ether - future or past I could not tell, I have no maps.

After Crich I had to press on, for my next destination lay well south of Derby. This I regretted, for I sensed I could be missing much in a superficially dull tract of the county. Egged on by the Morgan, I sped down through Bullbridge, crossing the remains of the lovely Cromford Canal and passing beneath the converging railway lines of Ambergate. At Heage I came upon a windmill. At Hartshay I crossed the A38 and turned right on to the Ryknild Street, an old Roman Road which led me to Horseley Woodhouse. There seemed to be some internal logic to my route, for I found my way with relative ease, mentally ticking off a memorised list of the commuter satellites which orbit around Derby and Ilkeston. Smalley, Stanley Common, West Hallam, the traffic was thickening, rush hour beckoned and the rural roads had become rat runs. The Morgan left them in a cloud of dust. Ockbrook, Borrowash and across the Derwent past Elvaston Castle Country Park to Aston-on-Trent. I felt as if I was fast-forwarding a video to get to a more interesting part of the story. I crossed the Trent at Swarkestone, negotiating the ancient causeway which marked the end of Bonnie Prince Charlie's Jacobite march on London in 1745. Swarkestone is said to be the longest stone bridge in England. It is three-quarters of a mile in length and parts of it are as old as eight hundred years, though the bridge which spans the Trent itself dates from 1795. Its continued use by large volumes of modern traffic

is astonishing. Yet one is somehow glad that it has not been by-passed by some ugly modern structure of steel and concrete and pensioned off for tourists to gawp at.

Have you anticipated where we are going? Calke of course, that great time-warp of a country house, only recently exposed to the nation's avid gaze under the auspices of the National Trust. As a member I did not have to pay to get in. I flashed my pass and the man at the entrance booth waved me through as if I was one of the Harpur Crewes in whose ownership the great house had been since it was built by an unknown architect between 1701-4. We had never been a family for stately homes until we were persuaded one day, at Chirk Castle, to join the National Trust. Sometimes the direct approach works. One is caught off balance and cannot think quickly enough to say 'no thank you'. Thereafter it seemed sensible to make as much use of the annual subscription charge as we could, and whenever we have had an hour or two to kill on holiday or en route, we have made a bee-line for the nearest National Trust property and derived much enjoyment thereby, not least because most of them feature excellent refreshment rooms and seemingly an agreement with Sam Smiths of Tadcaster for the provision of bottled nectar.

After that long, involved drive I was parched, and treated myself to tea and lemon cake in the sunlit courtyard before commencing my peregrination of Calke Abbey. Thirst quenched and hunger satiated, I began my tour with a video presentation shown in the old stables where horses once champed in their loose boxes. Where Calke differs from most stately homes, is that the National Trust decided to present the house more or less as they found it. The Harpur Crewe family were a dynasty of recluses and hoarders and over the years Calke had become a time capsule, an Aladdin's Cave of forgotten treasures in which the dwindling family eked out a twilight existence far from the beaten track of the world, far too shy to become involved with all the paraphernalia of public office to which most families of their standing aspired. When Charles Harpur Crewe died unmarried in 1981, his younger, equally unencumbered, brother Henry was faced with death duties amounting to £8 million attracting interest at the rate of £1,500 a day. The morality of taxing death has always seemed to me to plumb fresh depths of iniquity. We may envy wealth in others, but presumably it has been taxed along the way as it was acquired. Why should it be taxed again? But death and taxes are twin certainties and it appears that Charles, with a recluse's mix of innocence and arrogance, had not anticipated either.

Cornered, Henry (who, at the time, appeared to be living like an owl in the roof) offered Calke to the nation at an estimated value of £14 million, sufficient to clear the tax liability and provide funds for repair and maintenance by the National Trust. Unfortunately, the Treasury refused to accept that portion of the estate which was not defined as 'heritage' land. Two or three years of wrangling in high places ensued before Calke Abbey was 'saved' for the benefit of the Great British Public by no less a personage than the Chancellor of the Exchequer on the 13th March, 1984. It opened its doors to the outside world five years later. Five years of painstaking repair, though not necessarily renewal. Before work was begun, each room was photographed and every object catalogued, so that when the work was complete everything could be returned to exactly where it had been. To quote the guide book, above all else the National Trust wished to preserve the house's potent, but fragile, atmosphere of quiet decay. Moving from room to room, from floor to floor, I could only marvel at just how well they had succeeded. Of course, at home my family is quite capable of achieving an atmosphere of 'quite noisy decay' within hours of the house being spring-cleaned, but the achievement at Calke is on a different scale altogether, though I do sometimes wonder if, as a good father, I should be encouraging my children to take this sort of thing up professionally, given their obvious natural bent.

Whilst I have great admiration for the National Trust, I am not always convinced that the approach of their volunteers towards visitors is quite right. I imagine it is not an easy balance to achieve between intrusiveness and effacement, but it's a skill which needs to be honed. Sometimes you just want to stand in a room and look, but it's rather disconcerting if the guide on duty is staring intently at you as if: a) you're about to ask an amazingly intelligent question the like of which they have never had ventured to them before; or b) you're about to rip down the curtains (made to match those executed by ex Spitalfields weavers under royal patronage in 1857) and make off with them because they just happen to match the new sofa you've ordered from DFS on exceedingly favourable credit terms.

Most of the NT volunteers who people the rooms at Calke are, however, refreshingly good at their job. I made a mental note to mention particularly a sparky young blonde called Jo Carter who was rather good at explaining the rolled maps in the library, and a gentleman called James Dodge who hailed originally from Northamptonshire and who had corresponded with

J. L. Carr. Sometimes, though, conversation stalled and I found my gaze drawn through sashed windows to the high waving grasses of the surrounding parkland which, according to the guidebook, is found most conducive by beetles. In the drawing room my attention was drawn to portraits of Sir Henry Harpur (1763-1819) and his wife Nanette. Their's had not been a conventional society union - she had been a servant when he made her his mistress, and they had lived in a small house in the grounds before he married her formally in 1792. The headmaster of nearby Repton School had nicknamed Sir Henry the 'isolated baronet' and he was reputedly so shy that he frequently delivered orders to his staff in writing. I began to warm to such a character, feeling we had much in common. But it was half past five, the staff were growing restless, and I was informed that it was too late in the day to go looking in the grounds for the 'secret tunnel'. I braved the disappointment, acknowledging mentally that an hour or two was hardly enough to do justice to a self-contained world which had quite possibly defied all attempts by many a Harpur Crewe to map and define it.

I found myself on the A514 heading for Swadlincote. In my home town of Burton-on-Trent, which is in East Staffordshire, there is a tendency to think of South Derbyshire as a foreign land on the far side of the River Trent. Furthermore its inhabitants are widely considered to consist of a race of inbred and retarded nincompoops with whom one consorts at one's own risk. I must hastily add that I have never subscribed to this theory, having found South Derbyshire girls refreshingly uninhibited, and South Derbyshire lads as amiably disposed as I towards the most basic animal instincts of the football field. Besides, I have always felt a strong affinity with industrial communities, as if, in some previous incarnation, I had been a collier, or a potter, or a charabanc driver specialising in allotment society outings to the Lincolnshire coast. Post-industrially, it grieves me to relate, South Derbyshire's landscape has been ethnically cleansed, what passes for Progress has frog-marched through it, though here and there pockets of the past remain, throwbacks to when men were proud to be men.

One day in 1983 a Midland Red bus driver knocked on the virtually still wet paintwork of our newly opened publishing office and said he'd written a book called *Swadlincote Garage* which was about fifty years of motor bus operation in and around South Derbyshire. His name was Arthur Peto and we rapidly became good friends. He was a dapper little man, close to retirement age, and constantly harping on about his perceived inadequacies of contemporary bus operation. His book was not so much about buses - though there were plenty of photographs of beauties going back to the great days of Birmingham built D7s and S10s - but about the people who had spent their working lives at Swadlincote Depot: demon drivers, cheeky conductors, curvaceous conductresses, irascible inspectors, moody maintenance men. Even lists of services made a poetic contribution, routes like the 721 which operated from Coton-in-the-Elms to Donisthorpe Colliery (presumably carrying colliers in one direction and farmworkers in the other) or the 817 which ran from Swadlincote to Burntwood (facilitating visits to your relatives in the asylum). There were photographs of football teams and cricketers, outings and dances, long service awards and kiddies Christmas parties. A little world in microcosm. A busman's holiday!

Arthur's book sold well by our modest standards and, by word of mouth, spawned a whole series of nostalgic titles concentrated on the locality. In retrospect we were rather unbusinesslike to let such trade die away, but after two or three years of intensive publishing, it seemed as though the bubble had burst, and that South Derbyshire's thirst for local history had been quenched.

Publishing is not an easy business to be in. The up front costs are out of all proportion to the income derived. Not until you go to a reprint do you really see a profit and, if as is the case with the majority of titles, your publication doesn't capture the fickle reading public's imagination, you will have spent many months and thousands of pounds for no discernible gain. Furthermore, as an author myself, I found it difficult to meet the demands of my contributing writers. Anyone who has ever put pen to paper has a clear image in their mind of how their book should look, how it should be promoted, and where it should be stocked. In a perfect world it might be theoretically possible to meet with their demands. In reality disappointment and resentment - on both sides - is the inevitable conclusion.

Arguably the most surreal image, in a town of surreal images, is Swadlincote's ski slope. Switzerland comes to South Derbyshire. What the old miners of Granville Colliery would have made of this transformation scene is open to conjecture. When I was about fourteen someone told me that they still had a steam engine at Granville. Excitedly, I wrote to the area offices of the National Coal Board and got permission to visit the mine. Steam had all but disappeared from British Railways, but here on my doorstep, or so I thought, they were still using steam shunting engines. But it was all a misunderstanding. The foreman on duty welcomed me eagerly enough and led me into a high windowed building topped by a tall brick chimney.

"There she is," he announced proudly.

And there she was, not a shunting locomotive at all, but a stationary steam engine employed in raising and lowering the cage which took the miners from and to the various seams. Cower youth, I politely feigned an interest, thirty-five years on I truly would have fawned.

I parked the Morgan in a side road close to where the entrance gate to Granville Colliery used to be. What was once a cindery wasteground is now a green sward. In the middle distance the ski slope's chair lift and toboggan run occupy land once given over to the winning of coal. Amongst the Swadlincote Ski Centre's 'superb facilities' there's a nursery slope 'ideal for those who have not ventured onto the slopes before'. When our friend Angela Salt came up to stay with us from her home in the metropolis one winter weekend, she vocalised a wish to try out these 'superb facilities' for herself. Veteran of many a challenging French and Swiss piste, we awaited her performance with baited breath. Thus, we were naturally disappointed when she fell and injured herself on the ice in the car park, and

Mining to skiing, Swadlincote

A shadow on the tracks, Granville Colliery

was thereafter unable to demonstrate her prowess to its maximum effect.

Mere skiing is not all that Swadlincote Ski Centre has to offer, snowblading and tobogganing are alternative attractions, whilst for those who enjoy the social whirl of apres-ski, the licensed Alpine Restaurant offers raclette evenings, fondue parties and oompah nights. I can see by the way that you're looking at me, you suspect me of fractiousness. OK, humour comes at a knock down price in these parts, but I'm not trying to score cheap points, I just happen to have liked South Derbyshire as it was, wounded but romantic in its post-industrial decay. But hey, we have no choice but to inhabit 'our time' as one would an item of 'off-the-peg' clothing. We lack the wherewithal to ask history to provide us with 'made to measure' garments just to suit our outlook and demeanour. Thirty years from now, fifty-somethings will be telling their grand-children how wonderful Swadlincote was when it had a ski slope, of that I have no doubt.

The smell of fish and chips hung over Church Gresley - I imagine it always does. This is the home of Gresley Rovers, a plucky little non-league team who are nicknamed 'The Moatmen' because they play at the Moat Ground on Moat Street. Eden and I went there last winter and saw an exhilarating eight goal thriller with everything: penalties, sendings off, own goals, outbreaks of fighting between the players, and meat pies to die for. We haven't been back. Nothing can ever be as good as the first time. And as for the ground itself, it almost defies description. Everyone has heard of sloping pitches, but Gresley's pitch is not so much a slope as a series of hills and valleys resembling a hastily flung aside goal-keeper's jersey. Home knowledge, I imagine, is of great advantage, players being seemingly able to vanish from sight in the valleys before remerging to devastating effect on the hillock in front of goal. You can keep your overpriced Premiership with all its tantrums, it's at grounds like this where football's heart thumps loud and true.

The title of this chapter infers that we have come to journey's end, but this is not quite true. Sir Nigel Gresley, the railway engineer, is buried at Netherseal on the banks of the River Mease, right at the toe end of the county, and that's where I meant to end my day out in Derbyshire.

I dropped down from Church Gresley on to the A444 and made for Overseal. 'The 444' would be a likely entrant in the accolade of Britain's slowest road. Find yourself behind a slow moving vehicle along here, and you can forget your next appointment, and the one after that, unless that is, you gamble with an appointment with death. Driving back from a printing exhibition with my father and two colleagues one day in the Seventies, I happened to look directly ahead from the front passenger seat to see two beer trucks running parallel with each other and heading towards us at no little speed. From his angle in the driver's seat, my father obviously couldn't see round the bend like I could. I yelled at him to slam on the brakes as the two massive vehicles came round the corner. Just in time the outer lorry completed its murderous overtaking manoeuvre, and the two of them went insouciantly on their way. I don't recall ever having been so close to death in my life.

The Gresley family's connections with South Derbyshire go back to the Middle Ages. Herbert Nigel Gresley was the fourth son of the Reverend Nigel Gresley, the rector of St Peter's, Netherseal. His father was also the 9th Baronet Gresley and the young Herbert Nigel's existence must have been idyllically passed in the large rectory whose gardens run down to the banks of the Mease. He went to Marlborough - where he is said to have developed a flair for mechanical drawing - leaving the year that H. F. S. Morgan arrived. He was apprenticed by the London & North Western Railway at Crewe and got his first job with the Lancashire & Yorkshire Railway in Horwich. But Gresley's career really took off when he joined the Great Northern Railway in 1905. Six years later he became that company's Locomotive Superintendent, whereupon, on the grouping of the railways in 1923, he became Chief Mechanical Engineer of the London & North Eastern Railway.

But that dry catalogue of a career does scant justice to Gresley's genius. He was the designer of two of the most famous steam locomotives the world has ever known - *Flying Scotsman* and *Mallard* - engineering masterpieces but also works of art in their own right. As a trainspotter on York station, I can clearly remember seeing *Flying Scotsman* before it was purchased for preservation. With the acquiescence of its crew, I hoisted myself up onto the footplate for a moment or two while the great engine took on water. I saw *Mallard* at York as well, its streamline casing carrying a plaque to commemorate its world speed record of 126 mph achieved whilst hauling a test train south of Grantham in 1938.

Boys Own stuff, but now this great man lies in an unkempt grave in a country churchyard instead of with his equals in Westminster Abbey. You might, however, argue that he prefers it so, for often he would return to see his mother and go rook shooting. Recently the local authority have erected an interpretive board at the entrance to the cemetery, but the simple grave itself is uncared for. Aware of this sad state of affairs, I had stopped at a Tesco store and purchased a small spray of gypsophila. It hadn't occurred to me that there would be nothing to place it in. Each time I laid the flowers on the grave the breeze picked them up and blew them across the grass. I cast around for something to weight them down with to no avail. In the end I just let them to chance, sure in the knowledge that when night fell, and some great ghostly Gresley streamliner thundered through the graveyard, they would be blown away in its slipstream anyway.

Sir Nigel Gresley's grave, Netherseal

Horse Dealers - Willoughby-on-the-Wolds

There were travellers other than I on the broad-verged by-ways of South Notts that day. At Willoughby-on-the-Wolds I encountered a family of travellers, but I had driven by before it occurred to my rusty thought processes that their campsite would make a terrific picture.

"We were admiring your car," a woman called to me as I reversed up the road.

"I was admiring your horses," I quipped.

They were on their way from Appleby Horse Fair to Telford. The rest of us could make the journey in three or four hours via the M6. They were taking a week or two.

"You get to know where the horses can graze," she told me, "and we're not in any hurry."

That's the secret then, not to be 'in a hurry', only we're not very adept at taking it on board, rushing from one deadline to the next as if our lives depended on it - and of course they do, the banks and the building societies have seen to that. They were lovely folk, and didn't bat an eyelid when I got my camera out. In return I gave one of the children a ride around the block. When I got home that night Jackie and Tamar were aghast that the travellers had allowed one of their children to go off in a car with a total stranger. I don't suppose it had occurred to them or me that any danger lurked in the offer. If you live life on the road, beyond bureaucracy and the insecurities of modern society, trust must become instinctive.

We parted on good terms, they wished me well with the book, I wished them well with the next horse fair.

"You know where you're going then,' the woman called as I put the car in gear.

"I take each road as it comes," I laughed, and drove off to look for Nottinghamshire.

Of all the counties I covered for this book, Nottinghamshire is probably the one I know least well. Before the M1 was built my dad used to drive north on family visits to York and Tyneside by way of the Derby ring road, the Borrowash by-pass, Stapleford and Sandiacre, the Nottingham ring-road, and the White Post, on to the A614 past Ollerton to the A1. It was no more convoluted than most journeys were in those days. And sometimes, if you couldn't get away early, you'd have to stop overnight. That way Britain seemed a bigger place, and destinations, when at last

you reached them, of much different character and atmosphere to home, and thus more worth visiting.

And there, pretty much, you have the sum total of my knowledge of Notts, excepting many a winter Saturday spent happily with Jackie at the City Ground in the glory years of Nottingham Forest under Brian Clough and Peter Taylor, watching Robertson shuffle down the wing before dropping inch-perfect crosses for Woodcock and Withe to despatch gleefully into the opposing net.

So in most respects, this one day itinerary of the county was more exploratory in nature than the other, more nostalgically inspired rides in this book, and I began at Willoughby on the Wolds simply because I was used to seeing it signposted from the Melton road at Wymeswold and liked the sound of it. Don't signposts do that to you? Don't you find yourself attracted irrationally to the names of places you've never been? As if some defining answer might be discovered on reaching them - some instinctive circle squared.

"There were poppies in the fields, a sight I always associate, like pantiles, with travelling east."

There were poppies in the fields, a sight I always associate, like pantiles, with travelling east. They made pretty little crimson splashes at the corner of yellow cornfields which speeded me happily on my way. Wasn't Widmerpool the name of a northern city in a Graham Greene novel? Or am I thinking of a character invented by C. P. Snow or Anthony Powell? All this unnecessary luggage occupies storage space in my brain just as my loft is filled with books and magazines. But my now half a century old memory is just like that loft, in as much as nothing can be found when it is needed.

The real Nottinghamshire village of Widmerpool has a new sign, which I stopped to photograph, a great many villages having seemingly spent their millennium budget admirably, if not always imaginatively, on new signs. Pevsner's *Nottinghamshire* spells it Widmerspool, a mistake or a corruption? Anyway he draws our attention to the 'sumptuous' neo-Elizabethan hall, but that is masked from public view by woods, and, with no further reason to be delayed, I was soon

motoring on across two main roads and into the quiet country through which the Grantham Canal wriggles its way from its eponymous terminus to the Trent.

Canal restoration schemes are currently the vogue. Long abandoned routes which no one but anoraks and dreamers ever thought to see being made navigable again are all of a sudden being returned to use. Stunning engineering achievements such as the Trans-Pennine Huddersfield and Rochdale projects and the Forth & Clyde in Scotland are to be welcomed not only in leisure boating circles but as harbingers of urban regeneration. A comparatively modest restoration scheme, such as the rural thirty-three mile long Grantham Canal, would similarly bring the benefits of increased tourism to the Vale of Belvoir, but there are times when I can't help feeling that it's better to let sleeping canals lie.

I wished I had a copy of the *Shell Guide to Nottinghamshire*, the last one ever published in the series. I felt as if I was going into 'Indian Country' unarmed. Pevsner is usually too preoccupied with chancels and naves to allow his erudite focus to fall on anything as ephemeral as atmosphere. The church at Colston Bassett, he tells us, lost one of its aisles following the depopulation of the Wolds. I was more excited by coming upon a cheese factory specialising in the manufacture of Stilton. Mindful of my adventure with the Arbroath 'smokies' in *Railway Holiday in Scotland*, I was concerned as to the effects of spending a day on the floor of a motor car might have on the taste, not to say the hygiene, of any cheese I purchased to take home, but the friendly girl behind the counter assured me that it wouldn't be a problem. No, the only possible hazard to the cheese that she could foresee, lay in the danger that I might eat it all before it got home to my wife! Also at Colston Bassett, I crossed the River Smite and saw my first pantiles; a sure sign that I was heading east.

The Morgan and I rattled over a cattle grid and into Langar where I had been advised to visit an attraction known as Naturescape. Rather disconcertingly I followed the signposts to an industrial estate on the edge of the village, occupying what looked like the site of a wartime aerodrome. Surely some joke? But no, passing a mobile burger bar, and taking a turn to the right at the end of a concrete driveway, I came upon a little oasis of greenhouses and potting sheds whose business in life is the propagation of wild flowers. It was too early in the day for the premises to be open to the general public, but a kind lady, whom I'd ferreted out from the back of one of the outbuildings, furnished me with a copy of the company's *Catalogue & Growing Guide*. From it I learned that a family called the Scarboroughs have been at work since 1978 developing a forty acre farm engaged in the production of wildflower seeds, plants, native trees and shrubs. The catalogue read more like a polemic than a sales drive, as if spreading enthusiasm for wild flowers was more important to the owners than making money as such. There are over two hundred and fifty species of wildflower available as seeds or as plants in the catalogue, for collection at Langar or delivery by post. Even just the names make great reading: Lady's Bedstraw, Nottingham-Catchfly, Fox & Cubs, Monkshood, Pheasant's Eye, Restharrow, Teazel, Toadflax and Tormentil. Thank you Mr & Mrs Scarborough, my cheque's in the post.

I was thoroughly enjoying this exploration of new territory, even if I was beginning to feel a little like the late, great, irreplaceable Brian Johnston doing an episode of *Down Your Way*. My greatest difficulty lay in preventing myself from asking everyone I met to choose a favourite piece of music. "I would like Susan Maughan singing *James, James Hold The Ladder Steady* please", says Mrs Elsie Cresswell of Langar "because it reminds me of the day my late husband fell off the roof and broke his neck. How we still laugh at the WI - and the ink not yet dry on that new insurance policy ..."

Beyond Barnstone I crossed the little River Whippling. At Granby I encountered a large church ('The S doorway is E.E. with manifold mouldings of the arch') and a wide village green overlooked by two nice looking pubs, but it was too early even for an 'all-day' pub to be open. Before I got down to the A52 at Elton I saw some wide sweeps of the Vale of Belvoir to my right. The service at Elton & Orston railway station proved a meagre two trains in either direction, Monday to Saturday. I suspect Beeching overlooked its existence when he was busy running amok with his axe. Half a mile from either of its villages, there were no commuters' cars in the car park, just

The poppy fields of Langar

bees buzzing over the hedgerows and the distant sound of a tractor in the fields; a curious stillness lying in wait for a passing poet.

Somewhere in the back of my mind I remembered something about an old shop still functioning at Flintham. I drove once through the village in one direction then back again, but no sign of a shop. I pulled up outside a house where some builders were at work.

"Is there a shop in the village?" I asked tentatively.

"Not for the last ten years," came the reply with that guarded tone people reserve for strangers asking directions, as if they derive self-satisfaction from knowing something you don't know. In France they'd rush out with maps and voluminous local directories, and press you to partake of a glass or two of the local vintage with them. Here we just suck in and shake our heads. But we travel writers are made from sterner stuff, and I persisted.

"Some sort of old-fashioned shop," I continued.

"Oh you mean the *museum*," said the older of the two builders: "Well you've come to the right place, this is the man who runs it," he added, pointing to the owner of the house they were working on, who had just emerged from the side of the building. You see what I mean. If I had taken no for an answer, I'd have been half way to Newark by now. The man said

I needed to talk to his wife, but that I had better be snappy because they were just on their way out. His wife was called Sue Clayton and she melted when she saw my yellow car.

"I'm so sorry, but we're only open on Sunday afternoons," she said, "but if you want to telephone some time and make an appointment, I'd be happy to open up especially for you."

But I had promised myself, before taking off on these travels, that there would be no going backs, no second chances. It was going to be a 'Polaroid' sort of book where everything happened haphazardly and without forward planning.

"I'll try and get back," I said, but I think we both knew then and there that we were only being polite.

I don't think there's a nicer town in England - of its size - than Newark. I don't know it well, but what I do know is that it's the sort of place you can wander round for hours and not get bored. A decent secondhand-bookshop would be the cherry on the cake, but as I escaped with the contents of my wallet intact, I had reason to be grateful for the absence of one. I even resisted the charms of a stall in the Market Place dealing in railwayana. For a pound I could have had a button off a porter's waistcoat; for fifty I could have gone home with a railway telephone in a walnut case. This Market Place is the nub of Newark, socially and commercially. 'A joy to examine,' wrote Pevsner, and I heartily concur with his enthusiasm. This is no place to provide an inventory of the handsome and varied buildings which overlook what they claim - with dollops of municipal pride - as being the largest cobbled square in the country, but it would be remiss of me not to mention at least the Town Hall and Buttermarket and the old White Hart Inn at the other end of the square, an astonishing 14th Century timber-framed building which rather mundanely now houses a building society at ground level. In the final analysis, though, it's the atmosphere of the Market Place which makes it even greater than the not insubstantial sum of its parts.

Newark would be a worthwhile destination for its Market Place alone, but it also has a river running through it, not just any river, but the mighty Trent itself. Or so one is lead to believe, though, in strict accuracy, it is the River Devon which flows past the town centre, the main, unnavigable channel of the Trent lying a couple of miles to the north. Good use is made of the river for leisure, though sadly hardly any for freight. Trip boats depart

at intervals through the summer from an embarkation quay in the shadow of the castle. I saw an elegant old Thames steamer called *Sonning* awaiting its next cargo of day-trippers, whilst a smaller vessel, and not quite so good looking, set off upstream through the lock with a party of elderly ladies who looked as if they had been let out of some establishment or other for the day. They sat bolt upright at the little dining tables in the saloon waiting for a signal to start on their rolls and butter. I imagined that those rolls with their little packs of accompanying butter might provide the most cherished highlight of the day. "I wasn't fussed about the meat pie," Margaret confided to Mary on the coach home, "but the rolls and butter were delicious." Rolls and butter, rolls and butter; that's about as far as most of us get in life.

I didn't have time to find out about downstream, but upstream of the castle, I can confirm, it is possible to walk along either bank of the canalised river. Some hefty looking warehouses echo lost trade. Newark was noted for its maltings and breweries and, even after the advent of the Railway Age, the river provided much of the transport facilities required by these twin industries.

If you would like to know more about Newark's industrial past, I can heartily recommend the Millgate Museum. There I learnt that two of the town's best known breweries belonged to James Hole and Warwicks & Richardsons. Examples of their old bottle labels were on display. James Hole adorned their labels with illustrations of Newark Castle, Warwicks & Richardsons favoured big letters and bright colours, though their Milk Maid Stout featured a rather fetching maid balancing a couple of pails of milk on her pretty shoulders, the subliminal message in the advertising being that if you drank enough of the stuff you could easily imagine her walking home with you.

Incidentally, I have more than a passing interest in beer bottle labels, because the printing firm my father ran specialised in the mass production of such items up until the advent of the disposable beer can. Part of the top floor of the Millgate Museum is given over to an exhibition of elderly letterpress printing machinery and type-setting equipment. It took me back to my college days and beyond, to summer jobs in the printworks, and long days standing over a case of type, laboriously making up lines by the time honoured method of picking up single metal characters and arranging them in some semblance of grammatical order in a hand held compositor's 'stick'. The old terminology still comes back to haunt me on the computer screen:

Aspects of Newark
Top left: The Market Place
Lower left: Riverside Warehouses
Right: The Castle

Level crossing negotiations, Rolleston

upper case and lower case being the parts of the oblong wooden container where the type was kept. Each line of type was then dropped into a 'form', a sort of metal frame for holding a page together. It's mind boggling now to look back on how time-consuming the whole process of printing was, and not so long ago either. And yet the odd thing about computerisation, and all the speed it brought in its wake, is that books, by and large, are no better than they used to be. It is as if in speeding up the process of production, something has been lost in the equation.

The stately bridge at Kelham carries the A617 over the main channel of the River Trent. A previous bridge on this site was destroyed during the Civil War, and following hostilities, a bridge of boats had to hastily be erected to provide passage over the river. Second only to railways in my affection, rivers are the veins and arteries of landscape. There used to be a literary tradition of writing about them, following them from source to sea and exploring their hinterland. My shelves groan with such books, but their subject matter is no longer in vogue, and publisher's lists rarely feature river titles now, which is a pity, because journeying down a river is an ideal way of getting under the skin of any given tract of land.

'The stream invites us to follow, the impulse is so common that it might be set down as an instinct; and certainly there is no more fascinating pastime than to keep company with a river from its source to the sea.' The naturalist W.H. Hudson wrote those fine words a century ago, going sadly on to add that: 'this is not easy in a country where running waters have been enclosed.' He was not, however, inclined to be put off by landowners and fences. It was a river follower's duty, in his opinion, to make his way past all obstacles, undressing and taking to the water if necessary. I share his outlook if not his temerity. Gradually the authortties are coming over to Hudson's outlook. You can walk the Thames, you can walk the Severn; the Trent, unfortunately, is not always so easily accessible, especially on its upper reaches where trespass becomes a necessary evil if one is determined to explore the river's course closely.

With the Morgan this was not an option. 'Another time, another book,' I promised myself, skirting the grounds of Kelham Hall, a mansion designed by Sir Gilbert Scott of St Pancras station fame, an enormous Gothic pile now occupied by the Newark & Sherwood District Council whose business is tourism and regeneration; I put my foot down.

You would be disappointed in me if I had stayed on the main road to Southwell. It would not have been in character. Thus I bore left at Averham on to a by-road which led through Staythorpe to Rolleston. Rows of electricty pylons plodded across the fields from the site of Staythorpe's old coal fired power station. It opened in 1950, the first of its kind on the Trent, but closed in the early Eighties, a victim of power generating progress. I remember its sidings filled with lengthy coal trains which could be seen from trains passing along the Nottingham to Lincoln line, which George Stephenson had engineered in 1846. At nearby Rolleston Junction you could alight and change into 'The Paddy' a shuttle service to Southwell which ultimately ran out of steam in 1959. Race Specials used to be run in connection with meetings at the adjoining Southwell Race Course.

Naturally all this railway activity is in the past tense, save for the frequent service of modern Sprinter-type diesel trains, and this remains an interesting route to travel over, by virtue of its pleasant river valley scenery of long horizontal meadowland vistas broken vertically here and there by lines of poplar trees. For train buffs (bless 'em) there is added appeal in the retention of many traditional gated level crossings and mechanical signal boxes. I caused consternation at the crossing at Rolleston by coming to a stop too close to the gate which opened, much to my surprise, *outwards*. Much embarrassed, I reversed under the withering gaze of the keeper. I toyed with the idea of trying the gates at Fiskerton, but my confidence was in shreds.

"Are you reserved?" asked the car park attendant at the National Trust's new Southwell Workhouse.

"Yes," I admitted sheepishly, "that's why my analyst thinks it's good for me to drive about in a bright yellow car." Apparently not wishing to be drawn into further discussion, he waved me through, hastily thrusting a laminated voucher in my hand with a: "Show this to the girl in Reception."

I toyed with the idea of calling my analyst there and then, but I knew she'd be out to lunch, she always is when I call, whatever the time of day. I could feel a panic attack coming on. When the girl in Reception asked to see my National Trust Membership Card I had great difficulty prizing it from my wallet. In the end all my Credit Cards spilled out on to the floor, all seventeen of them.

"You could do some serious damage with these," the girl remarked wide-eyedly as she helped me to pick them off the floor.

"Purely collateral," I whispered in reply, "purely collateral."

But the Workhouse, you don't need me to tell you, was no laughing matter. People came here at the end of their tether, the last resort of the aged, the infirm, the illegitimately pregnant and the poverty-stricken. When it opened in 1824 (though then known as the Thurgarton Hundred Incorporated Workhouse) Southwell Workhouse was considered a model of its kind. It had been inspired by the ideology of the Rev. John Thomas Becher whose motto was, paradoxically, 'an empty workhouse is a successful workhouse'. Essentially, Becher designed his workhouses to be so unpleasant that only the most desperate would consider entering them. Inmates were divided into seven categories: Old and infirm men, old and infirm women, able-bodied men, able-bodied women, boys between the ages of 7 and 12, girls ditto, and children under 7. Able-bodied male entrants were given work of the most tedious and tiring nature, such as the breaking of stones, the chopping of wood, or the grinding of corn. Women were made to scrub floors, usually for up to eleven hours a day. When families entered the workhouse they were segregated by gender and age. Vagrants, or entrants into the 'casual ward', would be given food and lodging for the night in return for work.

An audio is essential if you are to derive the most education - I hesitate to use the word enjoyment - from a visit to Southwell Workhouse. The National Trust have chosen not to furnish most of the building, realising - correctly I feel - that a greater sense of the foreboding atmosphere of such institutions would be derived from leaving the majority of rooms empty. Through your headphones you hear a sequence of dramatisations concerning the unannounced visit of an inspector, and his interviews with the staff (who have their own secrets to hide) and the inmates. It is an effective conceit, and you can take your time by making your way from room to room and from floor to floor at your own preferred pace. Personally I found it all quite surreal watching well-heeled 21st century visitors loitering within these bare walls, while listening intently to their audio machines, where poorly dressed and equally poorly fed inmates had once stood listlessly day after meaningless day.

Towards the end of the tour you come upon a room that is furnished to represent the building's last years of use as council accommodation for the temporarily homeless. An eyewitness account of this period of the workhouse's history assails your ears while you regard the five closely spaced iron bedsteads with horror, for this was how we looked after disadvantaged and desperate mothers and children as recently as *1977*.

I discharged myself from the workhouse and went back to my expensive sports car. The gulf was sobering. The spiritual calm of a small cathedral town such as Southwell provided a redeeming balm, and boy did I need it.

"Nice Morgan," said a lady in the car park.

"It has its good points," I replied guardedly.

"I couldn't run away with you, could I?" she asked.

"But I'd know you only wanted me for my car," I said sadly, before we parted chuckling, pleased with our repartee.

Some accident of ecclesiastical history has endowed the small town of 'Suv-ull' (as the patois would have it) with an enormous minster. The effect is that of a fish dock providing berthage for a great liner. Along with Ripon and Beverley, it was a satellite of the See of York whose archbishops maintained a palace here until it was thuggishly reduced to a ruin by Scottish troops during the Civil War. I entered by the North Porch, 'donated' - as suggested - £3 for the privilege of having a look around, and parted with a further £3.50 for an admirably produced illustrated guide book.

Because time was at a premium I made straight for the Chapter House which is remarkable for the quality of its decorative stone carvings, the so-called 'Leaves of Southwell'. These examples of 13th century stone-masonry are outstanding, a profusion of foliage, fruit and flowers accompanied by animals and birds together with human and not so human figures. I particularly recall the image of a grinning demon astride a man's head, it brought to mind our local tax inspector. There are green

"When families entered the workhouse they were segregated by gender and age. Vagrants, or entrants into the 'casual ward', would be given food and lodging for the night in return for work."

Southwell Minster

men and angels as well. In fact, I began to suspect that this was not the work of masons at all, but some necromantic trick of petrification. I could continue cataloguing the Minster's inventory of misericords, lecterns, stained glass windows, gargoyles, tapestries and monuments. I could tell of my surprise in coming upon a little wall-mounted memorial to the martyrs of Katyn. I could even bring God into the equation, for I was given to understand that he occasionally has access to the church when the tourists have all gone home.

But it was time to be back on the road, with half of Nottinghamshire eagerly awaiting my appraisal, and I was soon motoring down Station Road, past a big red mill beside the River Greet, and quickly into open country, heading for Hockerton. Was it just coincidence that a board bearing the inscription 'No Tipping' should be vergeside where the road to Caunton crosses a little watercourse known as The Wink? These verges were wide again, I noted, and took my eye off the road ahead for a moment or two to admire a hawk hovering overhead. To keep the Morgan happy I turned on to the A616 for a mile or two. We got up to the legal limit - in eight seconds!

Soon, however, I was hankering after by-ways again, and made a right turn on to a lonely road which led to Laxton. An empty road is like a fresh canvas, a blank sheet of paper, anything seems possible. Breasting a rise, I was suddenly presented with wide views to the north-east, an horizon of power stations marking the course of the Trent. This was the sort of motoring the Morgan was made for, or so it seemed to me. That its puissant V8 engine could make mincemeat of other motorists, I had no doubt, but to amble along a country lane at forty miles an hour with the hood down and the scents of dog rose and elderflower wafting out from the hedgerows to tenderly caress one's olfactory senses marked the apothesis of motoring for me.

Peter Morgan would be horrified. He wanted the Plus 8 to be a thoroughbred sports car, not something you went shopping in. The model I was driving dates from 1968, and was launched at Earls Court that autumn. Its V8 engine, which owed its origins to Buick in America, could out-accelerate an E Type Jag. It just as rapidly became a fashion accessory for the bright young things of the Sixties pop scene. When Mick Jagger and Marianne Faithfull went to court for possessing cannabis they arrived in the Rolling Stones vocalist's bright yellow Morgan.

Laxton is unique in being the last village in England to embrace the open field system. A Visitor Centre explaining this Medieval method of farming and the reasons why it has survived in Laxton is housed in a building beside the pretty Dovecote Inn. Inside I learnt about crop rotation, the pattern of the farming year and the meeting of the 'Court Leet' which convenes each December to elect its Jury and to discuss matters pertaining to the farming year. It was nice to come unexpectedly upon a little pocket of old England that had avoided the great levelling process otherwise known as progress.

I crossed over to the pub and bought a mineral water and a packet of crisps and took them outside into the garden. I looked out over pantiled rooftops towards the impressive church of St Michael and its handsome clerestory. There had been a castle in the village once as well which Pevsner claims is the largest and best preserved Norman motte & bailey in Notts. Three waymarked footpaths of varying length encourage visitors to explore the village and its surrounding countryside to witness its agriculture for themselves.

Ollerton, I think I have told you, was a point of reference on my journeys north as a child. The main road by-passed the village and all I can recall is a railway bridge and a roundabout. But there was something in the lie of the land and the sound of the name which appealed to me, just as we respond to a face or a voice that others take for ordinary. Perhaps J. B. Priestley felt similarly, for wasn't the ravishingly beautiful heroine of *Let The People Sing* called Hope Ollerton?

We missed a lot, sticking to the A614. Ollerton village boasts a fine old coaching inn, a not uninteresting 19th century church and a watermill on the River Maun. I guess in the Fifties the mill would still have been hard at work. Now, at least, it's preserved and open to the public on Sunday afternoons as part of the attraction of a popular tearoom. I parked the Morgan outside Mike Maloney's butcher's shop and went in for a pork pie, having been lured by a sign proclaiming: 'champion pies at affordable prices'. Neither claim need concern the Advertising Standards Authority, and in return for the enjoyment I derived from that pie I will tell you that Mike also has branches in Warsop, Blidworth and Southwell, a pie-lover's pilgrimage suggests itself immediately.

Two doors up, an elderly gentleman peered out of his doorway with evident interest, but I couldn't tell whether it was the pie he was drooling

Mike Maloney's butcher's shop, Ollerton

over or the car. We got into conversation. He was car mad, it transpired. I offered him a spin round the block. He was much gratified. His name was Geoff Beadsmore. He had recently lost his wife, and I think our jaunt involved the turning of more than three corners. I hope so anyway.

The roundabout I remembered in open fields against a backdrop of spoil tips and colliery headgear, is now engulfed by petrol stations and fast food outlets. On the outskirts of Edwinstowe I came upon Thoresby Colliery, one of the last deep mines in the district, indeed in Britain. I was glad to see a mine still working, and the headstock wheels still revolving, and I turned off the road and drove half way across a field to celebrate with a photograph. This is the 21st Century and you could argue that there is no future, let alone dignity, in sending men into the bowels of the earth to dig for fuel, but the closure of so many mines has left a social vacuum in the district which has brought drug-addiction and crime in its wake. I would rather the disenfranchised and jobless had taken to the forest, Robin Hood style, and stolen from the rich to give to the poor, rather than give in to heroin, at least the Government might then take notice.

Beyond Edwinstowe I was deep in Robin Hood Country, looking nervously over my shoulder in case the outlaws were on my scent. When I was five I would quite like to have been Robin Hood, or rather Richard Greene the actor who portrayed him in weekly instalments on the television. Forty years later my son Eden was bitten by a similar bug after we'd all spent an enjoyable evening in the grounds of Shugborough Hall with Karen and Robyn Tanguy, watching a strolling group re-enacting great moments from the legend of Robin Hood. Man or myth? It hardly matters. Tourism in Nottinghamshire would be the poorer in his absence. Two journalistic maxims spring to mind: never let accuracy get in the way of a good story; and if he didn't exist, we would have to invent him.

Thoresby Colliery

Mr Straw's House - Worksop

The B6034 proved a nice empty road where the Morgan and I could get up a decent pace. It runs like a well shot Will Scarlet arrow through the green heart of Sherwood Forest. I was reminded of Cannock Chase, there were the same prevalent textures of pine, bracken and birch. I was guiltily conscious of my failings as a tour guide, for this is The Dukeries, that spacious and genteel region of mansions and estates. But I had no time for Clumber Park, another National Trust attraction, Mr Straw's House at Worksop was my goal. As advised, I had booked ahead, promising the voice at the other end of the phone that I would be with them by four o'clock, and time was moving on.

I imagine many people think of the National Trust in terms of stately homes, but there has been a move in recent years towards the preservation of much smaller properties which comes with a realisation that all types of buildings and all ways of life are worth saving for future generations. No.7, Blyth Grove, Worksop would, if you walked past the front door, appear to be an unremarkable Edwardian semi-detached, three-storey villa. Probably it would not have attracted the attention of the National Trust had not Mr Straw himself bequeathed the contents of the house to them. This is not as

strange as it sounds, one of the volunteers inside assured me that lots of people leave the contents of their homes to the National Trust, not because they feel them to be worthy of exhibition, but simply as a means of raising funds against their value. When they sent a representative to look over the bequest, however, what was discovered was a virtual time-capsule, a Pharaoh's tomb of undisturbed possessions and decorations going back over seventy years. The Straws, mother, father and two surviving sons, had been a close-knit family, and when the father - a Worksop grocer and seed merchant - died in 1932, nothing of his was permitted to be moved in the house from that day forward. William and Walter Straw's mother died in 1939, and the brothers' response was the same with regard to her possessions.

Against this background, I made my way up the path to the front door of No. 5, the reception for visitors. Making myself known, the young woman behind the counter called to a colleague:

"Ah, here's our Mr Mystery."

I was rather chuffed with that. It accorded with my mental image of myself, a romantic figure of international intrigue, quartering the country in a gaudy yellow sports car. I did nothing to disabuse them of their preconceptions, took my ticket with a polite, but enigmatic, hint of approval, and crossed to the other side of the room where the increasingly compulsory scene-setting video was being made ready for my entertainment.

William and Walter Straw took up where their parents left off, living as if time had stood quite still. Following his mother's death, William returned from London, where he had been a teacher, to look after the day to day running of the house, while his younger brother, Walter, ran the family business. Neither of them married. For forty years Walter cycled to the shop each day while William remained at home to cook and clean and garden. On Saturday nights William baked bread to his mother's recipe. On Sundays they went to church and sat in the same pew. They resisted progress. The house had no telephone, television or central heating.

No expert in psychology, it occurred to me that the brothers had taken on their dead parents' personae, and that the house had been left largely untouched so as to perpetuate the illusion. I think the saddest thing I saw, as I moved from room to room, was a pair of brightly polished dance shoes belonging to Walter, and I wondered how often he had fallen asleep wishing there had been a corresponding pair of ladies shoes dancing through his life.

No.7 was fascinating and spooky in equal measure. Yes, it was good to see all those old brand names, the old clothes, the old furnishings, the old decorations and wallpapers; the raincoats and the hats left hanging in the hall. I was reminded of childhood visits to elderly relations' houses on Tyneside where a similar atmosphere of timelessness pertained. But the very fact that the house is now a museum, underlines the fact that for the greater part of the lives of two adult men it was a mausoleum. Just like the Workhouse earlier in the day, part of me couldn't wait to get out. Before I left, however, there was one more matter to attend to. I had to sign the Visitor's Book. 'Very interesting,' I wrote and signed it 'Mr Mystery'.

There was no need for me to drive back through Worksop's burgeoning rush hour, I turned right on to the B6045 and made for Blyth. It was a pleasant drive, the sun warm on my back, the road ahead fairly innocent of traffic. I encountered a number of conifer plantations: one, it amused me to read from the map, known as the Hundred Acre Wood, though there was no sign of Winnie the Pooh. On a certain trip north, I remember my father making a point of telling my mother and me that we were using the Blyth by-pass for the first time. How proud we were of Progress then.

So I suppose on earlier journeys I must have been driven through this little town with its wide streets, coaching inns, and high-towered church. I did it scant justice on this occasion also, turning right before I had even entered the main part of the town and continuing with the B6045 across the East Coast Main line railway at Ranskill and on to Mattersey where a signpost pointing to a Priory caught my inquisitive eye. This Priory lay at the end of a long, pot-holed lane. Halfway along it I began to curse my curiosity. Suspension - and I'm sure they won't mind me saying this - not claiming any lofty status in the Morgan hierarchy of what makes a classic car. Indeed, I rather think that the kind of people who like to drive a Morgan rather relish the roughness of the ride, it helps convince them they are getting character for their money.

I bet you're anticipating that I got a nice surprise at the end of the lane, a ruin of Tintern Abbey proportions graciously overlooking a picturesque reach of the River Idle. You should know better, life's not like that, all I got for my discomfort was a ruck of stones and fallen arches. According to the rather terse information board I was five and a half centuries to late to see the Priory at its best. Much of it had been destroyed by fire in 1279 and by the time of the Dissolution it was occupied solely by a Prior and four disgruntled monks belonging to the Order of St Gilbert of Sempingham, the only entirely English order. It appears much of the

Mattersey Priory

fallen stonework was appropriated to build the neighbouring farmhouse whose outbuildings, I could see, were being converted for domestic use. I hoped the new residents would enjoy the view more than I did. It was a long way back to the main road, I can tell you.

The B6045 took me as far as Drakeholes, a little gathering of houses and an inn called the White Swan where the Chesterfield Canal passes beneath a slight rise in the ground by way of a tunnel, 154 yards long. Oddly enough, having spent (I pull back from writing 'wasted') half my lifetime researching and writing about canals, I must confess not to ever having come across the Chesterfield Canal at all. This is essentially my loss, for by all accounts it is a pretty waterway wending its way from nowhere in particular to nowhere in particular, a metaphor for most of our lives, and just my sort of canal. I had parked by the sharp bend in the canal at the south end of the tunnel when I suddenly remembered, in a blinding flash of deja vu that I'd been here before, and I mean really been here before, having stopped for a drink in the garden of the White Swan on the way back from a day out at Cleethorpes with a college friend and his wife and a short-lived inamorata. It might have been a brief episode plucked from someone else's life story. Aren't we all made up of cliched occurrences and hackneyed events? The real magic comes from being there, from just being able to breath.

Through avenues of chestnut trees, I drove through the estate village of Wiseton, crossed the canal on a hump-backed bridge and turned on to the Bawtry to Gainsborough road for a few hundred yards before bearing left into Gringley on the Hill. The suffix is certainly accurate. In the context of the flat carrs - reclaimed from marshland - which stretched ahead of me towards the Isle of Axeholme, two hundred feet up seemed positively mountainous. I took in a moment to savour the view, then let out the clutch and let the Morgan glide downhill.

Flat landscapes have a special appeal for me. I love the Fens with their black soils and big skies, and the Somerset Levels seen from the train between Bridgwater and Taunton. Here, too, I felt at home, or at least 'in sympathy' with the genus loci and sensed that the countryside was backing me into a corner from which I would find it difficult to escape. Consulting the map I could see this was true. Once past Misterton, the only place I could go, and still be in Nottinghamshire, was the riverside village of West Stockwith. And when I got there the Trent would prevent further progress. I felt like a fugitive in a Buchan yarn. What I needed was a small boat waiting on the tide to whisk me away.

When I first walked through West Stockwith in 1974, on a riverine hike from Gainsborough to Althorpe, the Trent was so busy with barges that one seemed to pass me every few minutes. Twenty-seven years later the river was sadly bereft of boats. I suppose I may have hit a bad time with regard to the state of the tide or the movement of vessels, but there appeared to be a reasonable depth of water and I know for a fact that gravel and sand barges still ply their trade on the river, though in nothing like the numbers in the past. I was lucky enough to hitch a ride on a barge called *Swinderby* in 1979, running empty back upstream from Hull to Dunham (between Gainsborough and Newark) to load another cargo from the gravel pits there. It was a memorable experience and it whetted my appetite for more barge journeys: Avonmouth to Sharpness, Birkenhead to Warrington, and Hull to York which proved timely encounters with a fast vanishing way of life. Should you come upon tattered issues of a magazine called *Waterways World* at some jumble sale or other, you may read my reactions. Then, as now, I fervently believed that freight should go by water and rail wherever feasible. Now I read of political lip service to these ideals with unconcealed cynicism and inner despair.

Upon such profits and losses, but mainly the latter, I cogitated whilst slowly downing a pint of Timothy Taylors incomparable 'Landlord' on a bench outside the Waterfront Inn. Directly in front of me the Chesterfield Canal bulged briefly into a wide boat-filled basin before locking down into the Trent. In the good old days big-sailed keels and sloops would come in off the river and transship into narrowboats here for the onward carriage of goods to Worksop and Chesterfield and points between. Now the trade is in leisure and correspondingly of less interest to the onlooker, even when the cabin tops are draped in prime cuts of female flesh. The only vessel of traditional lines in the basin was a rather fetching little wooden-hulled fishing smack. I pictured bobbing on the tide race out at Trent Falls, where the Trent and the Ouse get hitched and assume the alias Humber, and I envied its owner the experience. A blue and cream single decker bearing Haxey on its destination screen brought me back to terra firma. Its rapidly diminishing rear end informed me that it belonged to Isle Coaches of Owston Ferry. One day, I thought, it would be nice to make a series of journeys by bus on Britain's back roads. In the meantime I would just have to 'rough it' in a thirty grand sports car. Well someone has to!

Bereft of barges - the Trent at West Stockwith

Signpost, Belton-in-Rutland

Asfordby to
LEICESTERSHIRE
Ashby de-la Zouch

I came to live in Leicestershire at the tender age of two.
Things might have been worse - my parents had steamer
tickets booked, with which to emigrate to Canada, before I
was born: and I can categorically tell you that I would not
have relished being Canadian. People jokingly ask you to
name a famous Belgian, but being famous and being
Canadian is an oxymoron, and so I was grateful
that my parent's obvious wanderlust landed me up
in Hinckley as opposed to Hudson Bay. There I
lived from 1954 until 1961, whereupon we
decamped to Staffordshire; though the link with
Leicestershire remained by virtue of two years being
educated in Ashby de-la Zouch.

The Leicestershire of my childhood is a misty
place, an environment of feelings rather than facts,
a hall of mirrors, grotesquely devoid of focus, a
mildewed album of photographs which I half suspect
of having belonged to someone else. Hinckley could
have not been more surreal had it been Belgian. A self-
sufficient, self-absorbed town, chiefly known for making
stockings and dry-cleaning clothes. For the first five years
of our sojourn there we lived in a modest semi-detached,
bay-windowed house on the road to Ashby. Little by little
my father prospered as a printer and I can remember the
advent of the refrigerator, the television, the french-windows
and the car. Days of the week were easily identified by what
was for lunch. Tuesdays were my favourite because it was
mince and mashed potato and my father taught me how to

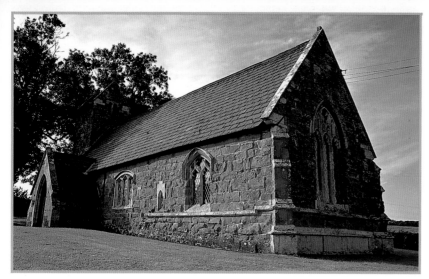

Welby Church

combine the two items into a fairly life-like representation of Ben Lomond.

On winter Saturdays we would go to watch the local rugby team put through their paces, and I learnt that 'hot dogs' were not made of Dachshunds, which were confusingly known as sausage dogs. A man there used to heave me up onto his shoulders and hurl me around. I was not enamoured, and have mistrusted extroverts ever since. We flew kites on Burbage Common, watched *Gary Halliday and The Voice* on television, and sometimes went down to the station to meet Scottish relatives off the train or hunt round the goods shed for displaced consignments of printing ink. I had a tortoise called 'Tommy', and our mongrel collie 'Eager' still bestrode my universe, if sorely missing his jaunts on Paisley's trams. All in all the world seemed a jolly place until the day came to go to school.

L. P. Hartley famously opened *The Go Between* with a line about the past being a foreign country. His words have been hijacked and misrepresented by hacks ever since. In one of my canal guides I rejoined: 'But there are cheap package tours departing there daily'. It was in this spirit that I ventured into Leicestershire, prepared to take the past on face value, assuming that the bricks and mortar I encountered were impervious to the resonance of re-evaluation.

And so in a lay-by on the outskirts of Asfordby I symbolically removed the hood from the Morgan, a Clark Kent kind of gesture, indicating the commencement of play; a gauntlet being thrown down. The lay-by was on a by-road which runs due north from Asfordby towards a place curiously called Ab Kettleby. I was surrounded by woodland and the early morning sun shone confidently through the trees, seemingly promising a nice day. So far I had been fairly fortunate with the weather on my journeys: not just for the sheer fun of travelling about with the top down, but also with regard to the importance of decent light for photography. Britain's irascible climate has caused me more disruption and disappointment in my working life than many a farmer, and you know how much they moan about the weather. It has become a tired joke in my family that I only have to take my camera out of its case for the clouds to roll across a hitherto unblemished, cornflower blue sky. I can set off for a day's photography in high spirits, encouraged by beaming television weather presenters assuring me that everything will be glorious, yet within minutes of arriving at my first location the sky will darken as if a sudden, unexpected eclipse had occurred. In my younger days regrettable scenes would ensue: the kicking of camera cases; the rhetorical questioning of certain religious figures' paternity; the flailing of fists in the direction of their supposed skyward abode; the strangulation of anyone rash enough to cross my path with fatuous inanities like "Shame about the weather, they said it would be such a nice day too". A trail of unsolved murders remains on the records at Scotland Yard. If only they had made the link between unheralded outbreaks of rain, and a certain travel photographer's movements, I would have been detained indefinitely at Her Majesty's pleasure.

Hood down, hat arranged at a jaunty angle, I accelerated away on a fresh adventure, looking forward to what Leicestershire had to display for my amusement and titillation. Skirting the perimeters of Asfordby's long forgotten ironworks and short-lived coal mine, I came to the lost village of Welby. According to my trusty *Shell Guide to Leicestershire* (by W. G. Hoskins, first edition 1970) the remaining church is of 13th century origin. It is a sweet little structure, and it positively gleamed in the bright sunlight. Hoskins opined that 'the interior is of no interest'. Just as well, because it was locked, though a notice advertised Evensong at 3pm on the second Sunday in the month, and if I had twenty-three days to spare I might have waited.

The coal mine precincts have become a business park, but then hasn't much of Britain become a business park, a steel-clad erection of numbing banality. Melton Mowbray reintroduced a sense of heritage and humanity. St Mary's parish church was chiming ten as I parked my car. First I had to come to terms with the ticket machine which wanted me to key in my registration number before it would issue a ticket. Naturally, the Morgan being relatively new to me, I had to walk back across the car park to ascertain just what that was. Then, on the way back to the machine, I was accosted by a member of the public requiring change, and in the conversation that followed I forgot the number and had to go back to the car again. Sometimes technology just gets on top of you, doesn't it?

Melton Mowbray *sounds* nice and pretty much fulfills its mellifluous obligation. Sadly, like all too many market towns, its thoroughfares are filled with charity shops now. To be a success in retailing, it seems, you must trade in purpose built precincts, preferably under cover. Only specialists can thrive in the high street these days. Dickinson & Morris are a good example. According to their excellent publicity material, they are 'the oldest remaining producers of authentic Melton Mowbray pork pies'. And not only do their excellent premises cater for visiting shoppers, they operate a worldwide postal service as well, so demonstrating that it is possible for shops of individuality to flourish in the 21st century.

Dickinson & Morris's shop is on Nottingham Street, and has been since one John Dickinson rented the property in 1851. The manufacture of pork pies is said to have gained popularity in the Melton Mowbray area as a by-product of the Stilton cheese industry. Whey left from the cheese-making process was used to feed pigs and a resultant surplus of pork was used to make pies. QED! A man called Joseph Morris joined John Dickinson's business in 1886 and in 1901 the Dickinson & Morris brand name was founded. Nowadays their pies are so well marketed that you can find them in most supermarkets. It is churlish of me to suggest that such widespread availability demeans their product, but popularity inevitably spawns vulgarity, and is the price of success. That said, I was unable to resist the immediate purchase of a pie, and, having made that transaction, its immediate consumption; though I would point out - if my mother is reading this - that I made a point of discreetly retiring up a side street to eat the pie, for I was brought up never, but never, to eat in the street.

I should point out that there are other pork pie makers in Melton:

Back-streets Melton - The Regal Cinema

Walkers on Cheapside; I. W. Knapp in Sherrard Street, and the butchers shops of Thompsons and Derek Jones in the Market Place and King Street respectively. I was being less than thorough in not sampling all their wares: I knew from experience just how tasty Walkers pies could be, and I suspected that quality might well be index-linked inversely with size of business, but the open road lay ahead and, as always, there was a good deal of ground to cover before I could put my feet up at the end of the day. Suffice it to say that you will also find shopping for cheese rewarding in Melton Mowbray.

Famed for pies and cheese, Melton Mowbray was once also regarded as the hunting metropolis of England. The territories of the Cottesmore, Quorn and Belvoir hunts converged on the town. Hoskins put it beautifully in the *Shell Guide* when he wrote that 'before the Second World War a thousand fine hunters were brought to Melton at the beginning of the season, and the night air was sulphurous with aristocratic adultery'. The phrase 'painting the town red' derives from a roisterous night in the town in 1837, when the Marquis of Waterford and his cronies ran amok in the town centre splashing red paint over anything - and anyone - they met in their drunken path.

Old railway viaduct - John O' Gaunt

Re-ensconced in the Morgan, I crossed the River Wreak - glimpsing a pretty reach thick with lily pads while waiting for the lights to change - climbed out of Melton on the B6047, and ascended into 'High Leicestershire', an empty, windswept neighbourhood on which what looked like an abandoned wartime aerodrome had found new use as an industrial estate. According to my one inch map I was already four hundred feet above sea level and still climbing. At Great Dalby I saw a brick built cottage with a corrugated iron roof and a Weslyan chapel dated 1846. Somehow or other I missed the church, for at home that evening I saw a picture of it in the *Shell Guide* which suggested it held much appeal. At Thorpe Satchville I saw a by-road going off to the left called Klondyke Lane which made me wonder what sort of gold-rush they had enjoyed there. What I do know, however, is that a Mrs Hillyard, England's lady champion of lawn tennis on various occasions between 1886 and 1900, once lived in the village. The village also boasts a rather nice looking old fashioned garage.

I pulled up in a lay-by to make notes beside the high-embanked earthworks of the old Great Northern and London & North Western Joint Railway along which trains used to trundle between Nottingham and Northampton until 1953, presumably after which time no one ever again made the journey between the two county towns. Writing lyrically and not a little nostalgically of its background in his 1973 book *The Forgotten Railways of the East Midlands*, P. Howard Anderson describes an undertaking of considerable character upon which, in Victorian and Edwardian times, special trains were run for the transportation of horses, hounds and huntsmen alike. Through the railway carriage window the dark patches of woodland which stood out amongst the paler greenery of the pasturelands had often been deliberately planted as fox coverts. One covert was called John O' Gaunt and it had given its name to a remote station east south east of the village of Twyford. John O' Gaunt was in the hunting territory of The Quorn. This was the countryside of Tom Firr, twenty-seven years the Quorn's chief huntsman, a national sporting celebrity in Victorian times as redoubtable as W. G. Grace. His diary of October 1879 records a sortie into the covert at John O' Gaunt succinctly thus: 'bagged a badger'.

Partly because I liked the sound of the name, and partly because I had glimpsed an imposing redbrick railway viaduct out of the corner of my eye, I turned off the B6047 and made for John O' Gaunt. The village proved insubstantial and disappointing, the viaduct anything but. I counted fourteen arches spread imperiously across a valley watered by a tributary of the Wreak. From a distance it seemed as noble as a Roman aqueduct and I was glad it had been spared demolition. So was the yellowhammer who regarded me quizzically from an adjacent hedgerow, or was he simply approving of the equally yellow metallic object parked so close to his nest?

The open road - near Launde

I hadn't intended to be side-tracked, but now that I had an opportunity to study the map I was taken with a spot called Launde Abbey and considered it my authorly duty to find out more about it for you. The Morgan concurred, and we set off again on our travels in high humour, purring contentedly along an unfenced road that traversed wide pastures grazed by ewes, some still maternally enamoured of a few late lambs. Clattering cacophonously over cattle grids we passed under one of the railway's old bridges - still intact despite half a century's absence of trains - and ran through the hamlet of Marefield where there were no mares that I could see but a donkey stud. In a nearby field a rather splendid looking bull with a ring through his nose thankfully displayed no apparent interest, let alone any stirrings of passion, towards the elegant yellow newcomer in his territory.

Thereafter each junction became a decision-making process, a potential twist of fate. An aromatic mix of engine oil and grassland assailed my nostrils as I let the Morgan make up its mind as to which direction to take. It led me to Owston. Body-guarded by beech trees which rustled in the breeze as I parked, the enigmatic church of St James appears to be the remnant of a one-time abbey. It shares its ochre coloured stonework with some gorgeous, to die for cottages and a gracious manor house. The highest point in East Leicestershire, Whatborough Hill, stands 755ft above sea level to the south of the village, just twenty feet higher than a neighbouring summit rejoicing in the name of Robin a-Tiptoe.

I had passed from a region where brick was clearly the indigenous building material into one where stone reigned supreme. Hesitating to over-quote Hoskins, I can't resist a line or two from the Introduction to the *Shell Guide* concerning 'rolling green hills, valleys dotted with little ironstone churches shining in the afternoon sun (and) a huge empty countryside with sign-posts pointing along by-roads to villages that were deserted centuries ago'. There is a Cotswoldian flavour to this ironstone, enhanced here by the loneliness of the landscape and its absence from any verge-littered and petrol-fumed tourist trail.

Launde Abbey, it transpired, is the Leicester Diocesan Retreat & Conference Centre, a large 17th century house erected on the site of an Augustinian priory. It stood in a tranquil parkland setting grazed by a freshly sheared flock of sheep, a mellow building redolent of ecclesiastical virtue, if not intrigue. But there was no reason to linger and so I let out the clutch and gave the Morgan its head on the high road to Loddington, where rooks cackled raucously from high trees and there seemed nothing for it but to veer left and cross the border into Rutland. A wayside signpost confirmed that Leicestershire was about to be left behind. Weatherworn and inclined to rust, it looked as though it had withstood the machinations of local government which had rendered

"The village was once notable for its corset factory which in its heyday employed forty women, one man and a boy."

England's smallest county obsolete in the crass Conservative re-organisations of 1974. Presumably the Highways Department overlooked its existence, though I prefer to think that insurgents within the organisation, members perhaps of a Rutland resistance movement, had spared it as a gesture of defiance, and now that Rutland has at least regained the dignity of a district, it can once again truthfully inform passing motorists of their topographic status, and there must be a moral in that - somewhere!

Not owning a copy of his *Shell Guide to Rutland*, I had left Hoskins behind at the border, but would have liked his knowledgeable assistance with Belton-in-Rutland, a delightful village of yet more ironstone dwellings with roses round each door. Uppingham lay just three miles to the east, and I was sorely tempted by the siren call of its secondhand bookshops, but time was marching on, so I went directly over the A47 into Allexton and turned left along a road I knew would bring me in due course to Eyebrook Reservoir.

You will remember, from Shallowford in Staffordshire, that my father was a keen dry-fly fisherman. New to Hinckley he made friends with Reg Wightman, a toy and sports shop owner who shared his enthusiasm for this gentlemanly pursuit, and the two of them would repair to Eyebrook Reservoir as often as their busy work schedules and/or wives allowed. The glittering array of Hornby and Tri-ang electric trains in his shop window elevated Reg to hero status in my eyes, and when I was old enough to acquire a reasonable boredom threshold, I was permitted to accompany the fishermen to Eyebrook, subject to stern conditions regarding the nature of noise abatement. Six or seven at the time, Eyebrook appeared as an inland sea to me then. I now know that it had been built to supply the water requirements of Corby steelworks just before the Second World War. In 1943 several Lancaster bombers used this massive sheet of water as a training area prior

to taking part in the Dam Busters Raid on the Rhur, much to the delight of the locals who gathered each night to watch the proceedings - one had to make one's own fun in those days. The potential of the reservoir for fishing was quickly recognised and it was soon being stocked with brown trout. My Dad and Reg must have landed their fair share of these in their day. From time to time I must have been handed a rod, but it was not a sport that captured my imagination. As we will see, I was much happier with the responsibility of rowing the boat.

Firmly back in Leicestershire, I found my way to Great Easton, another enchanting honey coloured village which, I was heartened to see, retained an excellent village store. The village was once notable for its corset factory which in its heyday employed forty women, one man and a boy. Soon after leaving the village I caught glimpses on the horizon to the north-west of Nevill Holt, a sizeable mansion (on the site of a lost village) which once belonged to the Cunard family of mercantile shipping renown.

In Hoskins' opinion, the large village of Medbourne 'is worth exploring on foot'. I almost complied, but though it sounds ridiculous, I couldn't find a parking space at the Nevill Arms, where otherwise I would quite happily have lunched, for it looked a gorgeous pub, a view reinforced by its regular appearance in Camra's *Good Beer Guide*. On such inconveniences do days revolve. I may have enjoyed too good a luncheon, and dallied too long by the highly delightful riverbank, spanned by a medieval packhorse bridge. Later I learnt that Medbourne had been a Roman settlement, whilst local lore has it that it was the site of the lost city of Medenborough, destroyed by a great fire. But instead of doing Medbourne justice, I crossed the Welland, had a brief but torrid affair with Northamptonshire, and found myself in Market Harborough for lunch at one of the clock.

Where to next ? - Eyebrook Reservoir

Symingtons Corset Factory - Market Harborough

The last time I arrived at Market Harborough I did so by boat. Historically I was in good company, because the fledgling Inland Waterways Association held their first National Rally here in 1950. These days the IWA are a rather respectable pressure group, and there's no doubting their credentials, but fifty years ago they were waging a guerrilla war against institutional indifference towards the canals and navigable rivers of this country. The association had been founded five years earlier by two remarkable but inherently different writers - Robert Aickman and L. T. C. Rolt. Aickman had written a fan letter to Rolt on reading his seminal account of a 1939 voyage around the midland canal network, *Narrow Boat*. It suggested the formation of a society to protect the inland waterway network from the philistines who would destroy it. At this distance in time I can only regard with amazement their achievement in getting the association under way. I could never find sufficient gaps in my writing schedule to commit myself to such time consuming work, and reading between the lines of their respective autobiographies, I think both men ultimately regretted the 'wasted years' selflessly given over to tub-thumping and administration when they were at the height of their literary powers. I know I would in similar circumstances.

The IWA's *Bulletin 22* announced: 'If available labour and resources permit, we hope to organise at a town in the Midlands a Rally of Members' boats and shore festivities'. The town they had in mind was Market Harborough which, as Aickman put it in his autobiography, *The River Runs Uphill*, 'virtually selected itself by reference to the waterways map'. This is perfectly true, but the *bon viveur* in Aickman was also aware that it was the location of a certain Three Swans Hotel, at that time presided over by the inimitable and eccentric John Fothergill, author of *My Three Inns*, a book as challengingly relevant to restaurateurs and hoteliers as *Narrow Boat* was to canaliers.

And so the scene was set for a *fete champetre* of stratospheric glory, an unrepeatable event impossible to replicate in time or space because all the ingredients would never be available in the same place at the same time ever again. It surprises me that no novelist or playwright has ever been inspired to dramatise the Market Harborough Rally. Not least of its appeal is the fact that Aickman and Rolt were by then in openly hostile revolt against each other, a Brutus and Caesar on collision course even as they espoused the same admirable ideals. Numerous sub-plots only serve to embellish the story: both heroes' marriages were on the rocks; sundry IWA council members were in revolt; and the Festival's cast list is positively littered with phantasmagoric figures such as the naturalist (and son of the Antarctic explorer) Peter Scott, the Director-General of the Festival of Britain Gerald Barry, the authoress Elizabeth Jane Howard, the artist Barbara Jones - I could go on, and on and on and, without being remotely disparaging, might add that it makes today's annual IWA rallies or festivals seem like caravan club conventions.

On reflection it is a great shame that Ealing Studios never picked up on the theme. One of their stalwarts, Hugh Griffith, - the engine driver in *The Titfield Thunderbolt* - was an acolyte of Rolt's and openly and significantly 'hissed' Robert Aickman at the prize-giving ceremony. I hope Tom Rolt was suitably embarrassed. He was my first canal hero; later I came under the spell of Aickman, interviewing him one afternoon in his South Kensington flat, conscious of being in the presence of A Great Man. So, in essence, I am neutral, and can only despair that their relationship deteriorated so rapidly, for it is a proven fact that antagonists are often the best bedfellows in enterprise.

My mind and my notebook are blank as to how or where I lunched in Market Harborough. Perhaps I went without, for this is often the case where work becomes too demanding or too exciting to spare time for such perfunctory chores as eating. I parked on Adam & Eve Street in the shadow of Symington's tall corset factory. In 1950 they offered tours to curious festival goers. Aickman professed to be underwhelmed, claiming to have experienced a greater *frisson* in the establishments of Parisian corsetieres; Barbara Jones exclaimed aloud that she couldn't see why women wanted to tie themselves up in such a way. Aickman joked that Symington's were 'in the pink' of health and trade, a reference to the plethora of pink coloured underwear in vogue at the time. Now what remains of their grandiose premises house council offices, the library and the town museum, itself devoting space to a former staple industry which manufactured such household names, in female circles at least, as 'Liberty' and 'Avro'. In World War II flippancy and frippery gave way to parachutes. Another branch of the Symington family made a fortune for themselves in the production of blancmange and soup. Captain Scott took their pea flour soup with him on his ill-fated voyage to the Antarctic. You can still buy Symington's 'Table Cream' on supermarket shelves, but it is no longer manufactured in Market Harborough. Both strands of this all-bestriding Market Harborough family are fondly remembered in the Harborough Museum and you can purchase postcards of Symington corsetry to send to your friends. I sent one to Karen bearing the witty inscription: 'Market Harborough or bust!'.

When we came here by boat in 1996, my family and I moored overnight in the basin at the top end of the town and strolled down in the evening to find ourselves a meal. Of course I wanted to make a pilgrimage to The Three Swans, but it was disappointingly bland and uncomfortably smoky. Moreover, they wouldn't serve food until seven o'clock, too late for our famished children and so we repaired to The Angel, not much different in ambiance but at least prepared to cook an hour earlier. I like to think that Fothergill would have made us more welcome. He was not an individual who suffered fools - still less customers - gladly, and, indeed, reading his books you cannot escape the impression that he would have made Basil Fawlty appear a sycophantic, fawning host of unbearable tact and obsequity. Fothergill bestrode his establishment in the guise of a Cromwellian officer. By the time of the 1950 Festival Aickman guessed that he must have been nearing eighty. He had owned The Three Swans since 1935. Catering is not a business for those who like a smooth passage and a neat balance sheet, and Fothergill's career was one long battle against debt and bankruptcy. He had begun his

working life as an artist, and then a gallery owner - he *knew* Oscar Wilde! Possibly he had too much strength of character to make an ideal caterer. Aickman summarised him thus: 'everything he did, he did with style, and therefore could not expect to be universally popular or loved' - though, of course, subconsciously, Aickman was probably writing of himself.

On one occasion Fothergill had a notion to enliven his menu by providing crossword-like clues to the nature of each dish. Perhaps fortunately, the well-known crossword compiler he sent his menus to for obfuscation died of a sudden (unconnected) illness before the deed could be done. Towards the end of dinner Fothergill was likely to emerge from the nether regions of the kitchen and walk between the tables of the dining room in order to ascertain the success or otherwise of his labours. An ideal reaction, he felt, would be for spontaneous applause to break out, as if he was an actor taking a curtain call. Sadly this goal was never achieved. Diners who dared quibble at the contents of their meals or the cost were likely to receive short shrift, those who appreciated that they had just consumed a work of culinary art were embraced as soul mates, Fothergill's sarcasm was as sharp and serrated as his steak knives.

What with all this business about the Festival and Fothergill I am guilty (as charged) of paying too much attention to the past, when I should be producing at least a pen portrait of present day Harborough. The *Shell Guide* stated in 1970 that it was 'a good town for pottering around the shops, some of them agreeably old-fashioned'. Thirty years on that feeling still holds good, and it is significant I feel, that both Hoskins and I should share a predilection for old-fashioned shops, by which I think we mean shops of individuality and character - irrespective of age - whose owners and staff display more than a passing interest in the requirements and general well-being of their customers, regular or otherwise. Bates the butcher and Hobbs the fishmonger on Church Square are two such establishments that I have been happy to advertise (gratis) in my *East Midlands Canal Companion*, and it would be nice to think that boaters from all corners of the world have felt similarly and silently thanked me for signposting them herewith. Their respective premises are overlooked by the soaring, limestone, broached spire of St Dionysius, Market Harborough's imposing parish church, itself adjoined by the town's startling old grammar school, a half-timbered building on 'stilts' which was apparently erected in 1614 originally in the role of a butter market, its curious design being 'to keepe people drye in fowle weather'. I

Honeypot Lane - Husband's Bosworth

guess it continues to fulfil that function, though on this warm, end of June, afternoon sandwich eaters were sheltering in its shade.

The Morgan and I took the Rugby road out of Harborough and motored through the upper reaches of the Welland Valley, the narrowing river marking the boundary with Northamptonshire. On trips to Eyebrook my father always used to remark upon a side-road in Husband's Bosworth called Honeypot Lane. I pulled in to pay it homage for auld lang syne. Halfway down it I discovered a cottage called 'Tunnel Farm' and was reminded that the Grand Union Canal made its way through the village in subterranean secrecy. I crossed that same canal at North Kilworth, being put in mind of L. T. C. Rolt's disappointment at encountering a countryside - to paraphrase his words - of untrimmed hedgerows, choked ditches and gates drunkenly leaning, whose husbandmen had abandoned their heritage for the get-rich-quick lure of industrial towns. In his foreboding he foresaw a drift to the towns which would irrevocably impoverish the countryside. But to put his fears in context it must be remembered that he was writing in 1939 before the war created an imperative need for every square inch of England's agricultural land to

be used to its full potential.

Throughout his writings, Tom Rolt is prone to such melancholic, Jeremiah-like outbursts. They are part of his charm: new is bad, old is best. For many years I was a fully paid up subscriber to this theory, but perhaps the wisdom of my half century allows me to see things less black and whitely. Were I to take Rolt's cue I could be driving the Morgan through North Kilworth and bemoaning the industrialisation of agriculture, the death of the village shop, the housing developments, however individually tasteful, that tend to overpower all that went before. Each age has profits and losses on the balance sheet of virtue.

Across the M1 I came to Lutterworth. Hoskins thought 'it had seen better days', an afternoon out with he and Rolt would not, I realised, have necessarily been a barrel of laughs. What they would have made of Magna Park, I shudder to think. It sits alongside Watling Street like a brave new world, a gargantuan conglomerate of distribution depots into and out of which processions of massive juggernauts ply a twenty-four hour trade. This, in my jaundiced view, is the real enemy now. Road as a mode of transport is out of control, the ever increasing size of vehicles out of all proportion to the width of the carriageways that they are driven on. The A5 is hardly changed from the road I was familiar with forty-five years ago when we thought ten tonners were bad enough, chastened by the death of a boy cyclist at Smockington. And now they are forty tons and more, and they hurtle down Watling Street at twice the speed, and children do not go cycling anymore.

A ruined monument at High Cross marks the meeting place of two great Roman Roads - Watling Street and the Fosse Way. One day towards the end of the Fifties, when they set about widening the road, we went up to see the man my father worked for, a printer and amateur archaeologist called Jim Pickering, rummaging about in the earthworks to see what the road-makers had thrown up. My mother and father's relationship with Jim and Wanda Pickering went beyond the formal bounds of employer and employee. There were social occasions a plenty - I particularly remember bonfire nights on Burbage Common - and their son, Guthrie, would sometimes come fishing with us to Eyebrook. Their daughter, Penny, was a vivacious girl with a shock of tawny coloured hair, and I can remember her making a bit of a splash at some party or other by wearing stockings for the first time. They were nice people to know and I am sure they helped my parents no end in the difficult business of bedding down in a new town - why even a new country in my father's case!

I'd arranged in advance to call in and see Jim and Wanda. I felt oddly detached about the prospect of seeing them for the first time in forty years. Indeed, the whole business of going back to Hinckley felt strange, as if it was someone else's past I was on the trail of, like looking for Jack Moeran's roots in Kington all over again. And if I felt odd, what must Wanda have thought, opening the door to a middle-aged man she'd last set eyes on as a nine year old.

"Michael, I'd have known you anywhere," she laughed. And the incredible thing was that I would have known her too, though I think she was being ever so slightly tactful! Jim came out of his study and he too looked exactly as I had remembered him. So I suppose this all says more about subjectivity and tricks of memory than a rational analysis of the ageing process.

What I really wanted to know from Jim, concerned the significance of High Cross. It caught my young imagination: we used to go picnicing along the Fosse Way in the vicinity of Brinklow, and in those days it was a barely metalled track along which the progress of a motor car was interrupted by the need to open and close farm gates, an enjoyable chore for which we children would receive a burnished penny. I don't know where Jim Pickering stands in the archaeological pecking order, but I do know that he has been at the forefront of the development of aerial photographic techniques in the interpretation of ancient land uses. His flying career is rather illustrious too. I was reminded of this as we chatted in his study, a well-ordered domain of boxed files and neatly-labelled photographic slide containers, decorated by numerous paintings and models of aircraft.

Jim was apprenticed to the family printing firm in the Thirties. To widen his experience he spent a year away in Sweden and Germany.

"I came back from Germany in 1936, convinced that Hitler intended war. By sheer coincidence the day I got back the formation of a new RAF Reserve was announced and, having always been interested in aircraft and flying, I joined immediately."

The Royal Air Force Volunteer Reserve was a sort of Territorial Army of the skies. For Jim it meant weekends spent learning to fly from Desford aerodrome and evening classes in Leicester. He is putting the finishing touches to a book provisionally entitled *RAFVR - A Narrative*. I for one

The flying archaeologist - Jim Pickering

can't wait to read it. When I used to read of WWII air aces in *The Victor* and *The Wizard* I can remember my mum and dad telling me that Jim Pickering 'flew in the war'. Something of an understatement, because he was a Battle of Britain Spitfire pilot stationed at Kenley, and then he was posted to Malta to fly *Faith*, *Hope* and *Charity*, the famous trio of Gloster Gladiators which held out against the might of the Luftwaffe until reinforcements could be sent. There followed a period in North Africa flying Hurricanes and Spitfires before becoming a test pilot. After the war he returned to printing, but it was not the end of his flying career.

"I remained in the Air Training Corps until I was sixty, flying out of Newton near Nottingham. But I also began to realise that I could apply aviation to archaeology, my two great interests. There have been about half a dozen of us studying what I call 'ephemeral phenomena'."

I am afraid Jim began to lose me at this point. He spoke of 'outlines' seen from above, 'ditches and field systems', 'moisture absorption', 'textures and patterns emerging from differences in the soil'. The photographs he showed me were easier to understand, if difficult to interpret by a layman. Equally, I could grasp how ideal, if not unique, Jim had been for the task, for all his photographs were self-taken on a hand-held camera whilst piloting an aeroplane. "It was all based on wartime experience," he modestly explained: "It was something you couldn't be taught."

It was quarter past three when I walked down Castle Street, Hinckley's main thoroughfare. I tried to remember where Reg Wightman's toyshop had been and where the record shop had been in which we bought my father a recording of Rachmaninov's *Second Piano Concerto* played by Moura Lympany. With the restricted knowledge of a four year old I thought the picture on the album sleeve was of my mother, who, or so it seemed to me at the time, bore a startling resemblance to Miss Lympany. It was at the same shop that I also remember purchasing several 78 rpm shellac discs which, when played back to back, contained a complete performance of *Sparky's Magic Piano*. Unfortunately the moral was lost on me, for in the story Sparky's piano had the ability to perform for him if he hadn't practiced sufficiently. But when I had occasion to try this technique with Miss Morrisey, my piano teacher at The Convent, we were met with a pregnant silence.

Castle Street seemed longer and less steep than memory suggested. I put this down to the optical illusion of pedestrianisation. Progress was slow, because I made a point of staring into the face of anyone I guessed to be in the region of fifty years old. Not so much with any thought of recognition, more to see how I might have looked if I had never moved away. Above one shop-front a plaque caught my eye. It marked the domicile, between the years 1879 to 1884, of one Mary Brame 'a prolific romantic novelist'. My ego, a pathologically shy character who positively shrinks from the public glare, sought reassurance from me that no such fate would befall us. From the withering look on my face he was able to judge that the chances were slim to say the least.

The schools were emptying, reminding me that at this time in the afternoon, forty odd years ago, I could be found walking Penny Briggs back to her home in Priestfield Road, before continuing alone to the bus station to catch a bus to Burbage. Now, instead, Arriva buses in ghastly turquoise filled the bays of the bus park where once my Midland Red double decker had graced the scene. I ducked into the Library and purchased a booklet entitled *Hinckley - as I remember it*. Unfortunately it harked back to an earlier period than mine, the Twenties, Thirties and Forties, sometimes the controls on these time machines are difficult to adjust. Apart from the traffic,

Regent Street was not unlike I remembered it. The premises of the High Cross Underwear & Knitwear Company recalled to mind a milk bar where we were wont to seek refreshment before attending a nearby cinema. What films spring to mind? *Bambi* and *Swiss Family Robinson* I'm afraid. 'Love is a song that never ends' - how true, how true ...

The United Reformed Church made me shudder. In my day, I seem to recall, it was known as the Congregational Church, and because church going was still the done thing in the 1950s, we went there with conscientious regularity until my father discovered the allure of the golf course. I am told that the minister called to enquire as to the reasons for our absence, and was informed that there was more chance of coming face to face with God on the golf course. Shortly afterwards, when we had moved from Ashby Road to Burbage, my name was put down for attendance at Sunday School, causing me to 'run away' and hide in the garage. The subject was not mentioned again.

Crestfallen, I was to discover that Pickering's had become a McDonalds - is nothing sacred? Behind the Union Inn I could swear there was a baker where we went to buy french bread hot from a deep oven recessed into the wall behind the counter. Walk beyond the bakery and you will collide with the Police Station where I nervously mounted the steps and approached the desk to enquire as to the whereabouts of my missing tortoise Tommy. In those days the police took such matters seriously, as though they were the equal of affairs of state. I do not hold the police responsible for his continued disappearance. I expect the unsolved case is still on record in the bowels of Hinckley's ersatz Art Deco Police Station - any day now there may be a breakthrough as fresh evidence comes to light.

I trudged up Stockwell Head to Wood Street, distinctly recalling my first morning at school as Adam must have regretted that business of the apple and the serpent. The horror of it haunts me, the institutionalization of children in the name of education, the homogenization of spirit and imagination, the wasted years, the mnemonic, stultifying monotony of exams. The only thing I can clearly remember learning at St Peter's Convent was how to make raffia place mats illustrating the Stations of the Cross, a technique I have yet to have need to fall back on in adult life.

The redbrick knitwear works that I walked past, clutching my mother's hand, was empty now, its windows balefully boarded-up. The escalation of fear as I passed it in 1957 was still tangible. There would be nuns at the gate

I was convinced. Genderless creatures sans hair, sans ears, sans facial expression; reaching out for me, as if some biblical sacrifice was about to be made. From the Congregational Church one Sunday to the Convent the next morning, no wonder I had my suspicions about organised religion from an early age, realizing even before the first cross of Ash Wednesday had been daubed symbolically on my terrified forehead, that it was all so much rigmarole targeted at those with the herd instinct of club members. Congregational to Convent? It might just as well have been the Philately Circle to Pigeon Fanciers Society .

But there were no gates, no nuns, no Convent. The gaunt buildings had been demolished. Replaced by bland modern flats. There had been a miracle. There had been a sacrifice. There had been a squaring of the circle. Not sure whether to laugh or cry, I walked back into town, remembering being knocked over on a zebra crossing on the way back into school from lunch one day, and the accompanying rush of children to the fence of the adjacent council school. They were to be disappointed. No gore. I picked myself up, brushed off the dust, brushed off the concerns of standers by and walked away - not from pride so much, more embarrassment. Self effacement starts early.

I turned the corner in my time machine. The shop where I used to buy threepenny slabs of Palm Toffee (favouring banana flavour) had become the premises of Magpie Antiques. I stopped to rummage through some books placed outside on a table on the pavement and came upon a few copies of something called *The Hinckleyan*. For a moment I assumed that it might be some local history journal, and began eagerly to flip through the pages to see if I might extract any nuggets of local life and lore with which to entertain you. Then I saw that it was the magazine of Hinckley Grammar School. I didn't even know that Hinckley had *had* a grammar school. And if that was the case, I thought with vexation, *why* hadn't *I* been sent *there*?

According to the contents of *The Hinckleyan* in my hand, in 1957 the Grammar School was a jolly place to be educated in. On the 21st of September the Hobbies Club were due to visit the Midland 'Red' Works in Birmingham, accompanied by Mr Jaques. On Bonfire Night the Sixth Form were due to be addressed on the subject of 'Ornithology' by the Headmaster of Albert Road Primary School. Two days later a performance of Mozart's *The Marriage of Figaro* given by the Phoenix Opera Company was to be given in the School Hall. On the 26th November Mr G. J. Rimmer, the Hinckley Gas Manager, would address the Sixth Form on 'The History of the Derivatives

Hinckley street scenes:
Above: Abandoned knitwear works; *below*: 'What kind of car's that, mum?'

of Coal Tar'. Now that's what I call a well rounded education, I thought, and went into the shop with a clutch of *Hinckleyans* in my hand.

"Oh these are selling like hot cakes," said the young woman as she emerged from the shadowy rear of the shop. "Everyone wants to see if their names, or their friends names are in them. Were you at the Grammar School?"

"No, I admitted shamefacedly, "I was round the corner."

"Ah, a convent boy," she rejoined, appraisingly. "They knocked it down two years ago. There was a big fuss about the bones."

"The bones?", I asked, mystified.

"Oh yes, apparently lots of nuns had been buried in the grounds and they had to advertise the bones, just in case any relatives wanted to come and collect them."

"That would never have happened at the Grammar School," I joked.

"No," she laughed, then said, as she glanced at the magazines before putting them in a bag: "But you were never at school in the Fifties, I don't believe it!"

I didn't so much drive as float out of Hinckley on the Ashby road, as flattered as a woman might be to be thought of as younger than was fact. Between 1954 and 1960 we lived on the corner of Ashby Road and Barrie Road. I was never sure if the latter was named after the dramatist or the Welsh seaside town by a Council Committee which couldn't spell. Across the road lived Mrs Dennison who had two daughters, one a blue stocking and one who was, mysteriously to my five year old ears, described as being 'no better than she should be'. She kept pigs - the mother that is, not the wilful daughter - in a small pen behind the grocery shop on the other side of Ashby Road, and it was my treat to go and feed them. I was pleased to see that the house was largely unchanged, though the stocking factory with its high chimney next door had been demolished and replaced by sheltered housing. The grocers had become Raj Stores and the owner of Indian descent was carrying boxes

of crisps through the door. My most memorable image of Ashby Road was when some road-workers set up camp outside, and a real steam powered steam road roller trundled up and down to my entertainment for a day or two of much delight. I can still see its black smoke fluming into the sky and hear the deep rumble of its passing.

We upped sticks from Ashby Road and moved to Beechwood Avenue, Burbage for the last two years of our time in Hinckley. Then my father got a position as Managing Director of a printworks in Burton-on-Trent. The odd thing was I remained in Leicestershire for my schooling. Travelling by train each day from Burton to Ashby de-la Zouch. And that's where I was pointing the Morgan now, powering out of Hinckley along the A447, the road my mother and I would journey aboard the stately double-deckers of the Browns Blue Bus Company on jaunts to Market Bosworth, or Earl Shilton or Coalville, barely containing our excitement at the thought of such exotic destinations. Invariably the bus conductor was a big man with a rubicund face which perpetually beamed. Who wouldn't be happy, my seven year old self reasoned, to ride all day on an omnibus with a rack of coloured tickets slung nonchalantly from one's shoulder together with a machine that tinkled like a bell when each ticket was ceremoniously punched in proof of purchase.

No true motoring enthusiast could resist the signpost for Mallory Park, which probably explains why I was perfectly content to speed by and turn off for Market Bosworth instead. Bosworth is a beautiful little market town 'charmingly unspoilt' according to Pearson's Canal Companion. Pevsner, on the other hand, bemoaned that the hall had been 'much interfered with in 1888'. One year my mother and I came to the Bosworth Show but spent most of the afternoon in the St John's Ambulance tent owing to one of her shins enjoying a slight altercation with a protruding tent peg. The 2002 Show was being advertised as taking place on 7th July. I would miss it by just ten days. I squeezed the Morgan into the last parking slot available on the cobbled square and tried to find a decent

"Who wouldn't be happy, my seven year old self reasoned, to ride all day on an omnibus with a rack of coloured tickets slung nonchalantly from one's shoulder?"

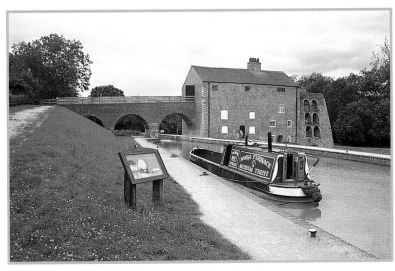

Moira - the Ashby Canal

Moira - the blast furnace

angle for a photograph, but all the other, aesthetically challenged cars of the twenty first century were in the way. No amount of juggling with modern traffic will let you make a street scene look good - ask any calendar or chocolate box lid photographer. Airbrushing is the only option, but I have not yet been tempted to cheat, and thus no picture of Market Bosworth adorns this book, which is rather a shame.

A silver Mercedes pulled arrogantly out of the Tennis Club on the road to Barton in the Beans. I have never liked tennis nor its strawberry-tea trappings and the pomposity of this haughty driver irritated me. I blew him away at the next bend, and for all I know he's still wedged between the uprights of the five-barred gate, wondering what hit him.

When we first moved to Burton I spent the first fortnight of the Michaelmas Term staying with John and Mary Wright on their small-holding at Swepstone. Each morning I would accompany their son Peter on the bus to school in Ashby, hoping against hope that it would be forced to wait at the level crossing while a mineral train from Measham Colliery plodded slowly across the B586 on its way down to the exchange sidings. In the evenings we would take tubs of food out to the cattle or search for eggs in

the hedgerows, the Wright's hens being apt to take literally the term 'free range'. It was an idyllic introduction to two largely blissfully happy years at the Manor House Prep School, and I was looking forward to going back there, but first I took a detour to the old colliery village of Moira which lies at the heart of the new National Forest.

I parked at Moira Furnace where a former blast furnace, built by the Earl of Moira in 1804, has been restored as a visitor centre and industrial history exhibition. The Ashby Canal, which had been abandoned because of subsidence in 1944, also runs here and has recently been restored with a new lock, something the original canal never had. Boat trips are offered now where horse-drawn, coal-laden narrowboats once glided by, their captains and their families the proud possessors of freshly purchased 'Measham' teapots. The blast furnace is imposing, though it was never very successful financially. Coal and clay were the commodities which made money for Moira. On my daily train journey to Ashby I encountered a still heavily industrialised community. The train slowed as it passed the circular kilns of the salt glazed drainpipe factory, the colliery sidings, and the Overseal engine shed in its triangle of lines, before pausing at Moira's black brick station, mostly to pick up yet more schoolchildren. They go by coach now of course, and the railway carries opencast coal, all the deep mines having closed down long ago. One of the last, Rawdon, has bequeathed its site to 'Conkers', a Lottery-funded 'hands-on experience in the heart of the National Forest' where you can 'see like a bat, touch a toad, or smell a badger: shop, walk, cycle or eat 'high quality fayre' at the 'beautiful licenced lakeside restaurant'. Me? I'd rather be down the mine!

To replicate my footsteps, I left the Morgan in the old station yard at Ashby. A cobbled approach road inset with tramlines which none of us could fathom. Years later I learnt that this was the terminus of the Burton & Ashby Light Railway, and became the proud publisher of a book on the subject called *Sixpenny Switchback*. To launch the book we hired a couple of venerable half-cabs from Stevensons of Uttoxeter and attempted to follow the course of the 3ft 6ins tramway on its wanderings through Gresley, Newhall and Swadlincote as closely as feasible. The book's authors, Joe Storer and Peter White gave a running commentary, and for a moment at least, all on board were transported through time back to the days when the young bloods of South Derbyshire would go spooning with their special girls 'across t' fields on top o' the car'.

In our day we railway children would have time to play cricket or football in the station yard before the train came to take us home. Occasionally it was possible to charm our way on to the footplate of the ancient Midland 2F which shunted the pick up goods. In winter, oblivious of any other passengers, mass snowball fights would take place across the platforms. And then there was Gillian, a snub-nosed, golden haired angel who had rapidly replaced Penny in my affections.

So life, you can see, was good for that ten year old, running with his chums past the Royal Hotel before turning right into South Street. Running not because we were necessarily late, but because in those days ten year olds ran everywhere, being as lithe as lynchpins and as fit as fiddles. Satchels bouncing on our backs, under the blue lamp of the Police Station we would speed, and on up to the entrance drive to Manor House School. On this occasion I did not run - not that there is not still some running left in me - nor did I take the school drive, but the one beside it, which leads to Ashby Castle.

To the pupils of Manor House, the most notable thing about the massive 15th century castle that towered over their school and its playground was the strangely advantageous thermals which enabled paper airplanes to stay aloft often for several minutes at a time. I am sure that even a fifty year old memory is not playing tricks on me when I tell you that I once got a paper plane to fly over the top of the eighty foot high Hastings Tower itself.

It was a good school and I was very happy there, apart, come to think of it, from the unwelcome attention of a bad-tempered teacher called Mrs Windybank, who made all our lives a misery. But in her classes at least, I learnt the hunter's art of concealment, the ability to sit through a lesson and not be noticed, let alone asked a question for which I had no idea of the answer.

A pleasant little blonde called Zoe sold me my ticket to see the castle and urged me to take an audio machine along. For once I complied, and it certainly came in useful, not so much as an interpretive tool, but as a prop - for with it clutched to my ear I could loiter by the fence separating the castle from the school and watch some boys playing junior cricket without drawing suspicious glances from the teachers in attendance. In the hysterical, paranoid world in which we live today, no adult can guiltlessly be a bystander to children's play without being suspected of paedophilia. As it was, in the guise of a tourist, I could steal surreptitious glances in the direction of the school with a clear conscience.

In warm sunshine I enjoyed my half hour exploration of the castle, and rather regretted that the school hadn't made more of its juxtaposition in my day. Curiosity satisfied, I went for a walk-about in the town, letting memories flood back into my mind, fleeting images of forgotten events and people. But forty years had elapsed and my focus was different. The boy had been indifferent to the graceful Georgian architecture of Ivanhoe Terrace, the cross erected in 1874 to the memory of Edith Maud, the stylish nuances of the Royal Hotel. Walking back towards the station I was brushed aside by a ten year old in short grey trousers and an old fashioned maroon coloured cap. He turned to apologise and there was a sudden flash of mutual recognition.

"Sorry sir," he said politely, with an impish grin.

"That's all right lad," I responded, "What's the hurry, you look like you've got a train to catch."

"I have," he grinned, turned and ran off again. And then I knew who he was, because the last passenger train left Ashby de-la Zouch in 1964, and I had recognised the initials embossed on the flap of his satchel - J.M.P.

Ashby de-la Zouch
Above: Tramlines at the old station
Above right: Manor House School
Lower right: The Castle

Fotheringhay

Flore to NORTHAMPTONSHIRE Fotheringhay

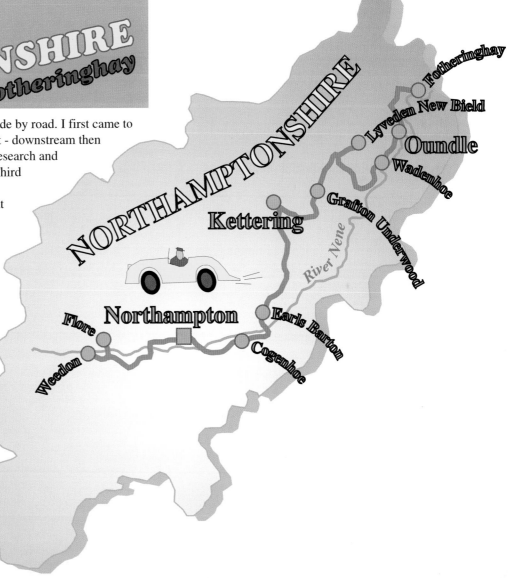

This is not so much a road journey as a river journey made by road. I first came to know the Nene in 1996, voyaging upon it by narrowboat - downstream then upstream - during ten days of hot August weather. The research and photography I did then went into the production of the Third Edition of *Pearson's Canal Companion to the Oxford & Grand Union*, but I was not the first to write about a boat trip on the river, because the naturalist, wildfowler and illustrator Denys Watkins-Pitchford had written more eloquently of his voyage along it in *Summer on the Nene* under the *nom de plume* BB in the Sixties.

I had BB's book beside me, along with the *Shell Guide* and *Pevsner*, not a bad line up to take along on a car journey, though a tad intimidating for those intending to follow in their literary footsteps. I was on the way to Flore, upstream of Northampton, and the day had begun damply. Only an optimist would have faith that the hood might be taken down on such a day. I was that optimist.

The traffic was nose to tail on the A45, lumbering along like a herd of mechanical elephants. The 'Please drive slowly through our village' sign seemed somewhat academic, whilst 'Support the Flore by-pass' posters appeared like an idea running behind time. So my spirits rose immediately as I turned down The Avenue, a sweet terrace of ironstone cottages. I cut off the ignition: pigeons were cooing, the traffic now, just a distant rumble. I drove a little bit further into the village and found an interpretive board which told me that Flore House dated from 1612 and the watermill from 1780. As for All Saints, the nearby church, it was substantial, largely 13th century in its origin and graced, according to Pevsner, with 'exquisite arcades'. For her part, in the *Shell Guide* of 1968, Juliet Smith had discovered that the font had once been pressed into service as a cattle trough. You will have guessed, however, that it was the mill which took my attention. The back road to Stowe Hill crosses the river under its high redbrick walls. Naturally it's residential now, that can only be expected. I leant over the parapet of the bridge and listened to the river plashing sadly below, as if lamenting: 'I'm here, I could work for you, why don't you use me anymore?'

From Flore by rights I should have driven east, following the river into Northampton. Instead, I doubled back to Weedon Bec to see one of the most unusual and unknown military buildings in Britain. At the beginning of the 19th century, when Napoleon was threatening to invade, the Government got out a map of England and looked for somewhere safe to hide King George III. Their gaze fell upon the tiny Northamptonshire village of Weedon Bec which, providentially, had just been linked to London by William Jessop's Grand Junction Canal. Here they built extensive barracks and a Royal Pavilion. An arm off the canal led into the Royal Military Depot through a portcullis. From the cynical perspective of the 21st Century, it all looks rather toytown now, its only remaining fortification a barrier, under the control of a security guard, which prevents the general public from closer inspection of what has become an industrial estate. George, I feel sure, would have rather been invaded.

Boaters on the Grand Union today find Weedon a good spot to 'drop anchor', for it has some excellent little shops, not least Brooklyn's grocery which dispenses fresh ham, eggs and pies. It was too early in the day to indulge my weakness for pies, so I pressed on, rain now drumming down on the hood, making my way back across the Watling Street, Northampton bound. Via Nether Heywood and Bugbrooke I found my way back to the A45. It is not one of the world's great romantic roads. Boxed between lorries, my view was restricted to industrial estates and retail parks: Wickes, Halfords, Matalan, Pizza Hut, McDonalds. I could have been anywhere. Not until I reached the rugby ground and the nearby offices of Northampton Corporation Transport, did I receive any visual reassurance that I was where

I intended to be. This bland approach has its antithesis in the Northampton Branch of the Grand Union Canal which descends from the main line at Gayton through a physically taxing series of eighteen locks which even a fit crew will take three or four hours to accomplish.

The late Ian Nairn, that extraordinary writer and broadcaster on matters architectural and town planning, drove into Northampton in his inimitable Morris Minor in 1972 on a journey by backroads from Marble Arch to Manchester televised by the BBC as one of a series of programmes called *Nairn's Travels*. It must have been a warm day (though one suspects that Nairn was prone to alcohol induced perspiration) for his trademark navy mac had been sacrificed for shirtsleeves. 'More like Belgium than any other town I know in England', he said, voice over, as the camera panned across a busy Market Square. And this was high praise from a correspondent who regarded Belgium as 'the most exciting country in Western Europe'. Nairn wore his architectural heart on his sleeve and rhapsodised over the market, drawing viewers' attention to the 'whole rhythm' of the square, and how 'the buildings come out fighting'. But he was in fear that the council were about to pull down its north side, in particular the Emporium Arcade of 1901, a strawberry cake building of balconies, gables and cupolas. 'A good neighbour' he called it, a building where 'things were always happening on the facade'. Inside the BBC cameraman revealed an Escher-like perspective of slopes and arches, and then Nairn was revealed on an interior balcony, listing the council's reasons for proposing demolition: they included the need for a new service road at roof level; the conclusion that the 'slightly seedy' shops within provided 'illogical use of a modern town centre'; that they had purchased the building for demolition and not investment; and that the arcade had 'no real architectural value'. 'No real architectural value', responded Nairn, anger rising in his voice: 'In my experience, which, with respect (heavy irony), is rather larger than Northampton Council's, this building is unique, and if this turns out to be an obituary, then I will be very sorry'.

I don't suppose *Nairn's Travels* was staple television viewing in the homes of town councillors - more *The Benny Hill Show* I imagine. So presumably their consciences were clear when they went ahead and demolished the Emporium Arcade in June 1972. Time has been kinder to their crimes than they deserve - it usually is where tyrants are concerned. Coming upon the Market Square now one is still made excited by its

Northampton Scenes
Top left: The Market Place
Lower left: Detail, 78 Derngate
Right: The Town Hall

vibrancy, and one is still reminded of Belgium. Survival of the Emporium Arcade would have been a cherry on the cake, but I still enjoyed walking between the tight-packed stalls in the rain, listening to the costermongers beseeching cries.

The elaborate Town Hall has Flemish overtones as well - 'assertively Gothic' in Pevsner's view; the work of Edward Godwin who claimed to be inspired by Ruskin's *Stones of Venice*. I found a suitable angle for a photograph and was much gratified by the appearance of an umbrella-wielding woman right on cue. You can prepare all you like for a picture, but more often than not it's a happy accident of light or interaction which lifts your work from the mundane to the inspired.

Whenever I'm in Northampton I can't resist walking down Derngate to pay homage and seek inspiration from what, if you don't concentrate, you might otherwise dismiss as an unremarkable 19th century terraced house. But No.78, is far from unremarkable, having been extensively remodelled by the Scottish Art Nouveau designer and artist Charles Rennie Mackintosh for the model maker Wenman Joseph Bassett-Lowke in 1917. Regrettably it is not open to the public, though in the Tourist Information Centre they told me it was due to open its doors in 2003. I can't wait!

78 Derngate is the only Mackintosh house outside Scotland. Bassett-Lowke's choice of a designer was inspired. Contact was made through a mutual friend. Mackintosh was living in Chelsea at the time and critics view the house in Derngate as the work of a reinvigorated architect and designer following a period when he had concentrated almost entirely on textile designs. Published photographs of the interior make your mouth water in anticipation of public access. Those of you familiar with the Mackintosh oeuvre will know what to expect. One may imagine Bassett-Lowke returning home from a busy day at his Kingswell Street works and letting himself into a completely different little world of magic and fantasy. By 1924, with his business doing rather well - particularly in the realms of O gauge model railway

equipment - the Bassett-Lowkes desired a move to a larger home. Ideally they would have liked Charles Rennie Mackintosh to design it for them, but by then he was a sick and ailing man and the work went to the German Expressionist Peter Behrens who created an equally astonishing house called New Ways on Wellingborough Road. One of Mackintosh's Derngate rooms was re-installed at the new address. In unusually eulogistic form Pevsner says: 'One does not know what to admire more, Mr Bassett-Lowke's discrimination in engaging Mackintosh at a time when his genius was no longer given adequate opportunities to express itself, or his courage in engaging Behrens, one of the earliest leaders of a new style of architecture then entirely untried in Britain'.

I could feel that the Morgan didn't like multistorey car parks. It was not comfortable in the company of rough, uncultured cars and mistrusted the attentions of leering attendants who dribbled all over its paintwork whilst astigmatically ascertaining that my time hadn't run out. The car greeted my return reproachfully, like a dog that had been left in uncongenial kennels. As far as its inanimate metalwork would allow, it seemed to jump up and lick me all over as I eased into the driving seat, making an 'I'll forgive you but don't let it happen again' sort of noise as I switched on the ignition. "Let's get outta here," I said, and we hit the ground floor - running.

It will take you half a day to get down to Earl's Barton in a boat. The Morgan and I did it in twenty minutes - the scenic way, through Cogenhoe. While I had parked to take a photograph of the village's admirable new millennium sign, a delivery van stopped to ask a man with a blind dog the way. Real 'Cooknoe' lies down a side lane at a tangent to the 'Cooknoe' of bungalows and council houses. Mill Lane leads down to the riverside. Just as I was getting back in the Morgan's good books we hit a succession of 'sleeping policemen'. I could sense it growing more irritable with each

"It will take you half a day to get down to Earl's Barton in a boat. The Morgan and I did it in twenty minutes - the scenic way, through Cogenhoe."

lurch. Over the weeks we had evolved a method of attacking the humps in a crab-like, sideways motion, which appeared to effectively minimise the chance of grounding, but I guess any onlookers must have assumed that I was driving under the influence of excessive alcohol.

We moored one night at 'Cooknoe' in 1996 and walked up the hill to The Royal Oak. It did not appear particularly salubrious from the outside, but they made us very welcome. Just as one should never judge a book by its cover, one should never judge a pub by its paintwork. The atmosphere inside was more like that of a social club, and we had the distinct impression that visitors were few and far between. I remember saying to the family, in what I thought were *sotto voce* tones, that the only thing which spoilt it was the piped music. When the landlord himself delivered our sizzling steaks he whispered in my ear: "Would you like the music turned down, sir?" I was too humbled to concur.

With Whiston's 'splendid late Perpendicular tower' soaring over my right shoulder, I turned the driving wheel to the left and crossed the river by White Mills Lock. The Nene's locks are characterised by guillotine gates at their tails. That is to say that instead of conventional mitred gates with balance beams, the 'gate' is raised and lowered vertically in a manner reminiscent of a French Revolution guillotine. Heads are just as likely to roll here too, not severed so much as exhausted, by the number of turns on the windlass handle necessary to operate the machinery. But the guillotines are part of the Nene's charm, and as I wrote in my guide book: 'You become accustomed to the layout of these locks, their operation and their idiosyncrasies'.

'Perhaps the most famous Saxon tower in England', enthuses Juliet Smith in the *Shell Guide* of 1968. John Gaastra, my art master at school, was equally passionate, and I had always harboured a desire to see Earls Barton's All Saints Church for myself, but the little shoe making town lies a country mile north of the Nene and I couldn't motivate the family to walk there and back from the boat - despite hints of a factory outlet. In the end, to complete my research, I drove there and was not disappointed. Prominent on a ridge overlooking the centre of the little town, the tower looks as if it might be made of an elaborate confection of praline biscuit fingers. In fact it consists of packed rubble, plastered over and decorated by pilaster strips. It has not been accurately dated, but, to quote the booklet on sale inside: 'the most widely canvassed date is 970'.

Six years after my first visit, I was glad to return. I walked up the diagonal path through the churchyard: diagonal, because it was thought that the devil could

Saxon tower - Earl's Barton

All Saints interior, Earls Barton

only travel in straight lines, and would thus be unable to enter the church. The doorway is Norman. Inside a woman was reading a book. She smiled and handed me a piece of paper, saying: "Use this to guide you round." She may have been of flesh and blood. She may have been allegorical. As I thanked her the church clock struck noon and I was treated to the chimes at close quarters, hearing the mechanism whirr within the tower. Saxon, Norman, Early English, Medieval, Georgian, Victorian, 20th Century; the church seemed less a conglomerate of masonry, more an organic structure with the capacity to reinvent itself in harmony with its time. From the booklet I learnt that it had only had fifty-three incumbents since 1221. Between 1747 and 1883 All Saints only had three vicars; two of them, father and son. Time doesn't appear to be in much of a rush in Earls Barton.

Some lyrics from a Paul Simon song came into my head, something about 'being here Lord and knocking at your place of business, but knowing I ain't got no business here'. And I began to think how odd it is that we take access to a church for granted, whether our visit is secularly or sacredly motivated. A church is a place of business, like a bank or a town hall. And despite the fact that banks and town halls are more likely to have a bearing on our lives now, we would not expect to have the run of them, which is perhaps a pity, for surely we could rely on a priest for more moral support than a bank manager or a councillor. I handed the interpretive sheet back to the woman and thanked her, telling her that I thought her church was very moving - she smiled, equivocally.

Back across the road Jeyes Pharmacy fulfils several functions: chemist, gift shop, tea room, stockist of dolls houses and accompanying accessories, agent for the Market Harborough Building Society, and location of the Earls Barton Museum of Village Life. The latter intrigued me. I came upon framed photographs of the Earls Barton Fire Brigade, the Earls Barton Baptist Choir, the Earls Barton Old Silver Prize Band, the Earls Barton Football Team and, 'shoeworkers on a break circa 1890'. One corner was given over to a display featuring Northampton's New Theatre. A poster for a show commencing 11th August 1958 proudly announced that Jack Gillam (Entertainments) Ltd would present the gay, glamorous, girlie show *Strip, Strip, Hooray*. It would star Cleo Romaine and Lynette Nibor supported by Renee Dymott (the unusual girl), Beulah Condon (the Windmill girl), The Clifts (sensational acrobats), and Rick Denby & Johnnie Grant, purveyors of modern mirth. Who'd have thought it of Northampton? A glorified strip club - and in the Fifties too! My imagination raced ahead through seedy matinees on damp afternoons, for the poster invited you to 'come when you like and go when you please'. I pictured bankers and businessmen, dentists and doctors surreptitiously making their way towards the

Yellow Cab? Kettering station.

Celine Dion comes to Kettering

New Theatre for a slice of the action. Suddenly I saw through the *double entendre* implicit in the first part of the salacious invitation and was stirred by pity for the lascivious treadmill upon which Cleo and Lynette and Renee and Beulah had found themselves upon; girls once pretty and vivacious who had excitedly answered adverts which promised the stars and gave them the gutter.

The Nene flows east through Wellingborough where, until 1969, narrowboats brought imported wheat from London Docks, having journeyed up to Northampton on the Grand Union Canal, and thence downstream. But the British don't make much use of rivers now for the carriage of goods. We prefer our road network, it's so functional, so utilitarian, so easy on the eye, so environmentally harmonious. I was following one of these roads, the A509, up the valley of the Nene's tributary, the Ise, on my way to Kettering. The dull drive was barely mitigated by a pretty church at Isham, a distant view of the Weetabix factory at Burton Latimer, and a burnt out car by the roadside which presumably marked the incendiary end to a joy-ride.

I parked beside the municipal Swimming Pool: via the Police Station

and the Magistrates Court I found my way to the Library; it seemed a symmetrical enough progression. The high Perpendicular spire of the parish church appeared to be puncturing a hole in the cloud-filled sky. On Market Street I saw my reflection in the window of the Blue Moon Bar. 'That's a chap who would be difficult to pigeon-hole,' I thought, 'either by age, or occupation, or intent'. So at least I had something in common with J. L. Carr, if not his genius. Self-described as 'a novelist and one-man publisher in a class of his own', 'Jim' Carr, like me, was dubiously saddled with the responsibility of concocting his own publicity, and it is naturally difficult to distance oneself from self-aggrandizement in the circumstances.

Carr had brought me to Kettering. Ideally I should have arrived by train early in the morning, as Peplow does Great Minden in *One Day in Summer*, his first novel, published in 1964, by which time he was 52 and working as a Headmaster at Highfields Primary School, Kettering. Carr was the son of a railwayman in North Yorkshire, and he writes felicitously of trains in a number of his novels, a not entirely uncoincidental attraction of his work where I am concerned. His best known novel, *A Month in the Country*, similarly begins in a railway setting, so does *The Battle of Pollocks Crossing*.

Both these novels were shortlisted for the Booker Prize, the former won the Guardian Fiction Prize, and was made into a film starring Kenneth Branagh and Colin Firth. It was the sort of film that the British make very well and nobody goes to see, often because the distributors don't deem it worthy of circulation on financial grounds. The same might be said of Carr's other seven novels. In the end he published them himself, in print runs of two or three thousand, beautifully made paperbacks whose imprint bore the message: 'This is a Printing Office, Cross-roads of Civilisation, Refuge of all the Arts against the Ravages of time. From this place Words may fly abroad, not to perish as Waves of Sound but fix'd in Time, Not corrupted by the hurrying Hand but verified in Proof. Friend, you are on safe ground: This is a Printing Office'.

J. L. Carr's novels are characterised by brevity, which goes some way to explaining their comparative lack of popularity with a reading public that equates worth with word count. *A Month in the Country* ran to just over thirty thousand words. But it is prose of almost poetic intensity which makes each word carry its weight, and a line in a Carr story can stay with you for almost ever, as when Joe Gidner, narrator of *How Steeple Sinderby Wanderers Won the FA Cup* recalls a romantic encounter on a raincoat under a hedge beyond the touchline: 'It was very enjoyable while it lasted. But afterwards, as always happens with me, I felt sad'. Perhaps, because of its football content and fenland setting, this is my favourite of the novels. Only Carr could have gotten away with the fable of a village football team winning the country's premier knock-out cup (and beating Glasgow Rangers of all the unlikely teams in the final) and made it plausible. In a beautifully produced booklet by Northamptonshire Libraries (H. E. Bates and John Clare are also covered in the same format) Byron Rogers notes Carr's twin preoccupations with comic fantasy and pessimism, which succinctly sums up the feel of a Carr novel for those still yet to experience the treat of reading him for the first time. At the back of this booklet a note refers to the J. L. Carr 'collection' held in Kettering Library, which explains - just in case you were beginning to wonder - what I was doing in the town.

Though I had six of his eight novels on my shelves at home at the time of this visit (and was soon to acquire a seventh - in Inverness of all places - soon afterwards), it was one of Carr's other talents as an illustrator that I had hoped to see as part of the collection. In seven huge volumes he had set out to record the county of Northamptonshire visually, a creative antidote to the sheer hard work of writing which I could all too easily empathise with, photography and cartography producing the same relaxation for me. Much of this work was undertaken on winter Saturdays, ostensibly, his son Robert (an archaeologist) has said, because he was not adept at painting trees with their foliage on!

Somehow or other I had it in my head that 'The Record' as Carr called it, was kept for posterity in Kettering Library. A willowy librarian called Rosalind (who might herself have stepped from the pages of a J. L. Carr story) unlocked the door to a store room for me, but couldn't exactly remember there being any books of paintings or illustrations. She rummaged through some filing cabinets in an unconvinced manner but came up only with some binders of press cuttings variously concerned with reviews, articles both by and about Carr, and biographical notes. At length a more senior colleague arrived and was able to confirm that The Record remained in private hands, but that I was welcome to leaf through the library's material, only could I do it 'outside' because the store room had to be locked for lunch.

So I sat with the usual suspects one finds in a public library in the middle of the day: the retired and the unemployed and the disenfranchised. I had a notion that 'Jim' himself might have been allowed back on 'day release' from the next world to keep me company. He might readily have been the man at the next table with his back to me, turning the pages of *The Daily Telegraph* so methodically. Though stymied illustratively, the material I had gained access to was full of fascinating nuggets. For instance I discovered that Carr had once sold a cricket cartoon to *Punch*; that he had explored the upper reaches of the River Ise by inflatable dinghy; that he calculated his income from novel writing averaged 17p an hour; and that we have in common the habit of keeping our business accounts in shoe boxes. Typically (because organised thinking is a personal failing) I have not yet mentioned that his main income from publishing derived from a series of hand drawn County Maps (Lincolnshire decorates our landing) and Pocket Books of sixteen pages, measuring five by three and a half - inches! Often the latter consisted of selections of poetry or the work of illustrators and engravers, but perhaps the most well received was his *Dictionary of Extraordinary English Cricketers*, an unlikely A to Z of the ridiculous and the sublime, the accurate and the outrageously invented. Thankfully J. L. Carr's son and daughter-in-law (who I once talked - with a mixture of humility and excitement - to on the telephone) continue to publish examples of his work from an address in Bury St Edmunds. Kettering Library even had a selection of some of the Pocket Books available for purchase, and I added eight titles to my collection at a cost of £1.25 each.

My car park ticket was rapidly running out of time, and I meant to head out of Kettering without further delay. However I was unable to resist poking my head into the Alfred East Gallery. Curiosity is an admirable trait in guide book compilers, but it isn't half time consuming. East was born in Kettering in 1844. After attending the local Grammar School (where his talent was recognised but not encouraged) he worked for his brother's shoe business. In 1874 his brother made the mistake of sending him to Glasgow as the firm's Scottish representative. Alfred enrolled in evening classes at the Glasgow School of Art (ha, the Mackintosh connection, you're right!) and soon couldn't resist attending full time. Over the next thirty years he travelled extensively in Britain and Europe and he quickly became established as a landscape painter of huge popularity, being knighted in 1910, three years before his death. Out of affection for his birthplace he offered Kettering a selection of his works, and they have been housed here ever since. How can I convey them to you? Corot springs to mind, there being more realism in his painting than, say, the French Impressionists, who were to some extent his contemporaries. Among the works permanently held in Kettering are a number of locally inspired scenes: *Midland Meadows*, for example, an oil painting exhibited at the Royal Academy in 1895 which depicts a scene at Tansor on the River Nene near Oundle, and *The Rising Storm, Billing Bridge*, watercolour of the river on the outskirts of Northampton. It was a nice little gallery, but of course I was in too much of a rush to do it justice. On the way out I had a sudden thought and asked the girl at the counter if they had any J. L. Carr's in their collection, but the answer was no.

It was high time I high-tailed it out of Kettering, but there was one last item I wanted to visit, so I drove the long-suffering Morgan down to the end of Station Road to take a quick look at the railway station, an attractive example of the Midland Railway's *fin de siecle* styling, said to be the work of Charles Trubshaw. The Booking Hall is of terracotta, the platform buildings in timber with lively ridge & furrow canopies supported by extravagantly scrolled ironwork. Two expresses in the teal green colours of Midland Mainline whooshed by while I stood in admiration of the architecture, and for a moment I felt like a J. L. Carr character hanging around for a plot to materialise.

The Morgan and I had to find our way back to the Nene. We pulled in by Wicksteed Park (where the nuns used to take us on coach trips, interrupted by a succession of halts for 'girls' of both sexes to be sick on the verge) and consulted the map. A bucolic route of double-barreled nomenclature was democratically decided upon which would take us via Barton Seagrave, Cranford St Andrew and Grafton Underwood. It was, as the Morgan said pointedly, 'nice to be moving again'. Then I stopped to take a photograph of a row of thatched cottages, and the silence was telling.

Grafton Underwood is every Hollywood film director's mental image of an English village. The thatched, limestone cottages look as if they've been hewn from Stilton cheese, and a brook busy with ducks accompanies the road from one end of the village to the other. It's a strange coincidence that I was made to think of Hollywood, because Grafton did become a little bit of the U.S.A. for the last three years of the Second World War. Seven Northamptonshire airfields provided American homes from home during the Second World War, and Grafton Underwood was one of them. Indeed, B17 Flying Fortresses flew the very first and very last United States Army Air Force missions from Grafton Underwood in August 1942 and April 1945, on the railway yards at Rouen and the Skoda works at Pilsen, Czechoslovakia respectively. I could make an attempt at humour here, and say that the raid on Pilsen didn't prevent Skoda from developing their range of motor cars and marketing them in Britain, but as a former (proud) owner of not one, but two Skoda cars, I would stand accused of bad taste in more ways than one.

There are two permanent reminders of the American presence in Grafton: a granite memorial stands at the end of the old runway, and a stained glass window in the parish church of St James the Apostle commemorates the men who were stationed here. To see the stained glass you have to collect the key from Quentin Bland at the Post Office. Quentin has lived in the village for all of his sixty-one years and can just remember attending children's parties at the air base towards the end of the war. Perhaps this explains his passion for the subject - he is the 384th Bomb Group's official British historian.

"Do you get many ex-servicemen visiting the village?" I asked.

Grafton Underwood

Left: Stained glass Flying Fortress memorial window
Right upper: 384th Bombardment Group granite memorial
Right lower: Interior, St James

"Not as many as used to, he replied, sadly, "you see they're all dying off now."
'Ah yes, there's the irony' I thought, 'war didn't get them but age has'.

The memorial stands alongside the road to Geddington, half a mile outside the village. Fifty-seven years after it had closed, there were still tell-tale signs of the aerodrome in the surrounding fields. As if on cue a Flying Fortress emerged from the clouds, rumbled over my head, and landed in the wheat nearby. I watched the crew extricating themselves from their aeroplane, noisy in the relief of reaching base. I could just make out the name under the cockpit. *Butcher Shop* it read, and rang a bell. Wasn't that the plane that Major Paul W. Tibbets had flown from Grafton Underwood on 17th August 1942, leading that first operational raid on Rouen? Tibbets went on to make an even bigger imprint on history, being the pilot of a certain B29 called *Enola Gay*, which dropped a certain sort of bomb on a certain Japanese city on a certain day in 1945. I was tempted to call over the hedge to him, some sort of soothsaying intervention, but realised it would do no good, history cannot be tampered with.

I should have continued a further couple of miles along that road to Geddington where there's a well preserved example of an Eleanor Cross, but in my ignorance I crossed the A6116 at Brigstock, destination Lyveden New Bield, a National Trust property four or five miles west of Oundle. I found myself on a lonely road negotiating a windy plateau, an ideal location, I expect, for the Welland Gliding Club who operate from premises near to another wartime memorial, this time to the crew of a crashed Lancaster. The National Trust ask you to leave your vehicle by the roadside and to walk along a much-puddled clay track for half a mile or so. What seems at first an imposition turns out to be a subtle exercise in stage management, a filtering out of the residual dregs of the present day. I began to whistle through sheer *joie de vivre*. A 'sea breeze' sighed through the neighbouring poplars. Even the sadness of a 'set aside' field could not dampen my spirits.

Lyveden New Bield belonged to Sir Thomas Tresham, a persecuted Catholic nobleman of the 16th Century. For Tresham, buildings represented much more than their face value. It was as if he was stating, for posterity, his beliefs in masonry and mortar. Perhaps the most bizarre building associated with him is the Triangular Lodge at Rushton, to the north-west of Kettering, but the house at Lyveden New Bield is astonishing because it is not a ruin as such, but an unfinished building where work ceased four hundred years ago on the death of its instigator. 'Sir Thomas Tresham's delight, skill and misfortunes are all epitomised in Lyveden New Bield' says the National Trust guide. It is built in the form of a cross and symbolically decorated with

Lyveden New Bield

devices and inscriptions which celebrate the Passion of Christ. It was intended to be an appendage of Lyveden Old Bield, a portion of which survives in private ownership near the road. The plan intended that the two properties would be joined by a sequence of formal gardens, some of which survive.

After flashing my National Trust membership card at the custodian I was shown around the building by a Collie dog, whom I strongly suspected of being Sir Thomas, reincarnated. We crunched from gravel-floored room to gravel-floored room until my companion's attention was diverted by the sudden fluttering of a pigeon - presumably a former servant. A spiral staircase took me to an upper floor whose windows offered intoxicating views across the countryside, to what the guidebook lyrically described as 'the billowing expanses of the gentle Northamptonshire landscape'. What a marvellous house it would have been to have lived in, had it ever been finished.

A heron flapped ponderously away from the moat, breaking the spell, and reminding me to go and have a walk around the grounds. They proved every bit as entrancing as the house, most notably a series of ornamental moats, or canals, along which it was envisaged guests would be promenaded by boat to view the gardens. I could see them as Sir Thomas might have hoped to have seen them: gracious ladies and gentlemen, serenaded by minstrels, the tinkling of laughter, the dripping of wet oars, whirlpools in

Four centuries unfinished - Lyveden New Bield

the placid, emerald sheen of the moat. Now, sheep graze where the formal garden was to have stood, and the scene reminded me of a French canal. Correspondence dating from 1597 has revealed that Sir Thomas was planning an orchard, and, after a gap of four centuries, the National Trust are going to make sure his wishes are carried out. Rare varieties such as Winter Queenings, Catsheads and Old Worcesters will be joined by pear, plum, cherry and walnut trees. That Collie, I was convinced, would enjoy himself to the full.

I could have been in Oundle within ten minutes, but I wanted to go to Wadenhoe, where, in 1996, we had moored for lunch at the King's Head - warm baguettes of beef and cheese, if my memory serves me well, washed down with Adnams bitter. There was also a dovecote in the village, its subfusc interior invigoratingly cool on that simmeringly hot August afternoon. It was only two miles away to the south-east on foot, through Lilford Wood, but in the Morgan it was an eleven mile drive. Even at my advanced age, I wager I could have beaten the car had I run across the fields. Between the ages of thirty-five and forty-five I was a reasonably fit half-marathon runner. These days I don't seem to get the time to do more than six or seven miles, once or twice a month. Like most of us, I work harder and harder all the time, just to stand still. It transpires that all that business about a future of boundless leisure was just a mirage. I pulled in outside Watts Stores in Aldwincle for a bottle of pop and a chocolate bar. A nice old fashioned shop, a proper village store. Mr Watts himself served me, admiring the Morgan through the doorway, but not wishing to swap places with its driver.

"Thirty years, I've run the shop, and my Dad before me, I just love the village life, I've never thought of going anywhere else."

Back in the car, a welcome breeze blew through the thin, post-harvested remnants of my hair, a refreshing distraction on what had become a humid afternoon. Sometimes it's disappointing to go back to somewhere you enjoyed visiting, simply because all the ingredients which flavoured it so appetizingly in the first place - people, or weather, or mood, or circumstance - are not guaranteed to be in place. By now the sun was sulking behind thickening layers of oppressive cloud. In 1996 Wadenhoe's cottages of stone and thatch had positively glowed in the sunlight. Now they glowered, like faces where sudden frowns have replaced a smile. But I was pleased to see that the Post Office was still in business (albeit on Mondays, Tuesdays and Thursdays

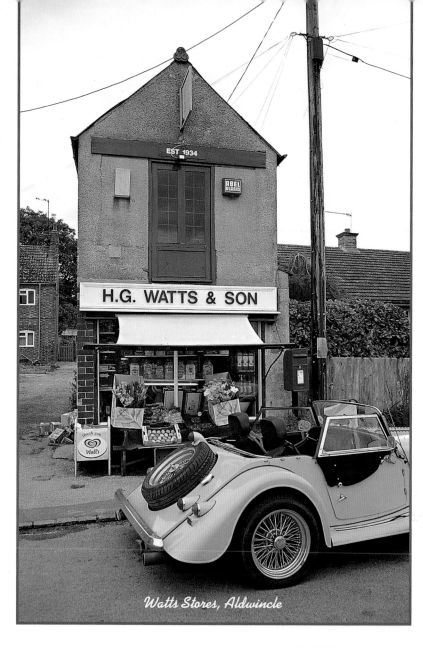

Watts Stores, Aldwincle

Wadenhoe - Telegraph Office and Dovecote

only), and still nostalgically advertising itself as a 'Postal Telegraph Office'. Apparently this was one of the first rural telegraph offices in the country, largely because the local landowner was Chancellor during Disraeli's term in office, and relied on close contact with Whitehall from the wilds of Northamptonshire. I wanted to try and get a photograph of the Morgan in juxtaposition with the dovecote, and somewhat cheekily reversed the car

into the walled yard where the dovecote stood. That old feeling of plunging out of heat into a cool, dark pond was absent on this occasion, but it was still pleasant to be back inside this early form of convenience store, as reliable a source of nourishing food as any deer park, rabbit warren or fish pond. As well as its potency, the circular dovecote at Wadenhoe retains its 'potence', that is a rotating wooden pole with a ladder to facilitate access to each nesting

Le Mans start for the post - Oundle

Limestone and yew trees - Oundle

box. Making sure the door was closed firmly behind me, I tiptoed back to the Morgan, half a dozen warm white eggs concealed in my pocket.

Like a shy person who relies a drink or two before becoming gregarious, Oundle needs sunlight to bring out the best in it. Little holes in the cloud were beginning to loosen its tongue. I arrived just in time to have a look around Geraldine Waddington's secondhand bookshop which excels in illustrated books. Of all things, I picked up a copy of Pevsner's *Nottinghamshire*. Two counties too late as far as my travels were concerned, but a worthwhile reference tool in retrospect. According to the fly leaf its first owner had been Jean Shenstone of Abingdon, and it had been purchased on 25th January 1962. I wondered idly what Jean's interest in Nottinghamshire had been: was she an architectural student, had it been her home county, was she planning an elaborate tour in search of boxed pews and carved lecterns? I always try to remember to sign and date my books as well, noting the place of purchase too. By winter firesides it's nice to remember when and where a book was bought. And when I have gone to that heavenly

'Hay-on-Wye', and my books are scattered to the four winds, I like to think they'll all go to a good home where someone else will value the names and the topographic predilections of their previous owners.

On our 1996 boat trip we developed a taste for the local wine merchant's house white. Amps live down an alleyway off the main street, and there I headed to see if I couldn't get a bottle or two to take home to Jackie. But the young man behind the counter shook his head. "We stopped bottling it two or three years ago," he said, "it was never very popular ..." The curse of popularity distorts everything, exaggerating the worthless whilst at the same time condemning that which is truly worthwhile to obscurity. "We still do the red," he offered hopefully, but I was already gone.

'During term time sudden invasions of young people coincide with breaks between classes, welcome surges of gaiety and insurrection at odds with the usual decorum inherent in Oundle's creamy coloured thoroughfares' - thus did I describe the atmosphere of Oundle in my *Oxford, Grand Union & Nene Canal Companion*. Most of the school and its houses is tucked away from the public eye, so that it's quite possible to go shopping in the town without being aware of its famous and ancient public school at all, until these sudden invasions occur. It has always seemed to me the sort of school that one would be proud to be an old boy (or girl now, of course) of, and it is not all public schools that it is safe to say that of. Sir Peter Scott (who we came across previously in Market Harborough) was educated here, and so were - I was charmed to learn - Peter Morgan and Charles Morgan - scant evidence to prove my theory, but reassuring all the same.

In 1996 we moored overnight in Oundle, tying our boat to the riverbank upstream of Oundle Bridge and throwing out gang-planks to facilitate the rather tricky passage ashore. We wanted to have dinner at The Talbot Hotel because Jackie and I had enjoyed a sumptuous Sunday luncheon there twenty years previously, but they weren't serving an evening meal until seven o'clock, they said, and the children in our party couldn't wait. Instead we ate at a charming little Italian called San Giorgio on West Street, and had a thoroughly enjoyable meal, both in terms of culinary quality and atmosphere. We wandered back through the churchyard as dusk was falling and the lights were coming on, and it seemed as if Oundle was a little toy town where everything ran smoothly and everybody was happy ever after. Back on board the boat, we were in bed before nine chimed, not stirring again until the dawn activities of ducks and moorhens disturbed our beauty sleep.

I suppose the highlight of our river journey, though, was Fotheringhay, a place which had always had a special magical quality for me ever since hearing Sandy Denny's eponymous song on Fairport Convention's *What We Did On Our Holidays* album, released on the Island label in 1969. *Fotheringhay* the song concerned the imprisonment, and subsequent beheading, of Mary Queen of Scots at the long since demolished castle. That savage act would have been reason enough for Fotheringhay to be remarkable, but it is also the location of one of the most beautiful churches in England. On our boat we first saw it from the bend in the river below Perio Lock. It was a sunkissed late summer evening, and the church's graceful lantern tower glowed incandescently in the light of the lowering sun like a benediction in stone. The local farmer charges a couple of pounds to moor beside the riverbank at Fotheringhay, but it's difficult to begrudge the money when you can stay in such a lovely setting. When night fell the church was floodlit. I don't think I can ever remember a better mooring overnight in twenty years of inland waterway travelling.

In any other car it would have been impossible to escape a feeling of anti-climax, but there was as much pleasure to be derived from easing the Morgan through the village as arriving by boat. My visit coincided with an exhibition in the church of Fotheringhay's 'Royal Connections' in honour of the Queen's Golden Jubilee. It meant that I had to pay to get in but it was worth it. A man with a Lancashire accent sold me my ticket and a copy of a booklet chronologically listing Fotheringhay's royal visitors. I am sure it was the sort of list J. L. Carr would have revelled in. My appreciation of history is still at the Liebfraumilch stage, but it is obvious that Fotheringhay was a nodal point for royal comings and goings - not to say intrigue - throughout the Middle Ages. Inevitably, one corner of the exhibition was given over to the gruesome events of February 8th, 1587. Every schoolboy used to know that it took the axeman three blows to sever Mary's head from her body, and that when he came to lift the head to prove to those assembled that the deed was done, it transpired that the hair was a wig which he held aloft in bewilderment while the head rolled away. They knew how to entertain themselves in those days, now we just watch television.

We had heard good reports of the food at The Falcon Inn and strolled up through the long grass below the church in anticipation of a hearty dinner. But it was Monday, the young barman pointed out indifferently, the chef's night off. The distaff side was not amused and retired to her berth in a sulk of Mary Queen of Scots proportions. The rest of us ate Pot Noodles. Sometime in the six intervening years, the inn appears to have had a change of direction, and looks like a restaurant now. I sat irresolutely in its car park, wondering if I should stay for dinner, but then decided to drive back to Oundle and try The Talbot Hotel. I got there just after six. Guess what - "I'm sorry sir, but we don't serve bar meals until seven o'clock, but there is a little Italian restaurant down the road."

"Don't worry, I know it," I said with a smile, wondering why I hadn't just gone straight to San Giorgio in the first place. When I got there they served me within ten minutes, a mouth-watering Carbonara. Just the thing to wind up a wonderful day in an inexplicably underrated county.

A roads which have been reduced in status to B roads are imbued with an aura of melancholy, like a middle-aged wife abandoned by her husband for a younger model. Not that such callous treatment necessarily spells the end of a useful life. Sometimes, the whole cathartic experience can have a liberating effect, a chance to begin again. This was how I felt about the B5493, formerly the A453, the one time trunk road between Birmingham and Nottingham. Enjoying its wide open spaces, the Morgan and I sped easily along, passing wooden bus shelters at the intersection of country lanes, which I somehow doubted saw much use in the depopulated countryside of North-east Warwickshire.

For some reason hard to fathom, I found the planning of an itinerary through Warwickshire more difficult than all the others. No clear route leapt from the map, though I poured over it for hours one wet Sunday afternoon, trying to imagine how places might look under the sun, listening to Rachmaninov's all but forgotten *4th Piano Concerto*, devouring steak pies washed down with a chill Italian white whose name now escapes me, though almost water-clear in its glass, a distant cousin of Frascati. Perhaps I knew Warwickshire too well, at least from the perspective of a canal boat. Marston and Hawkesbury, Braunston and Napton junctions, these are its nodal points in my mental gazetteer. In the Morgan I would need to reassess the shape of the county, make the most of the opportunity to explore beyond the claustrophobic confines of 'The Cut'.

No Man's Heath seemed a good place to start, a road-side hamlet whose very name reflects the uncertainty of its allegiance. Even the pub hedges its bets, being known as the Four Counties: and surely you don't need me to tell you what the other three are! I wondered

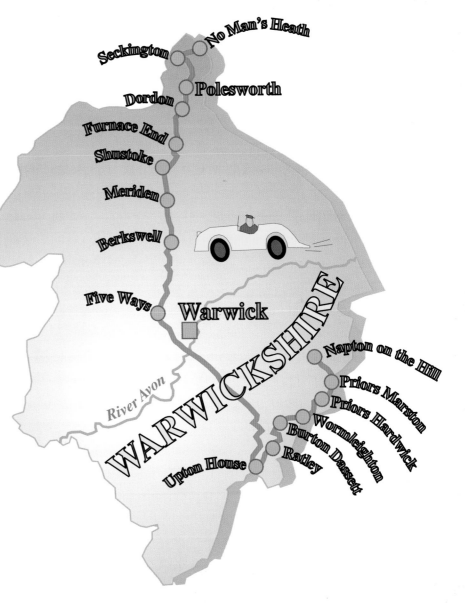

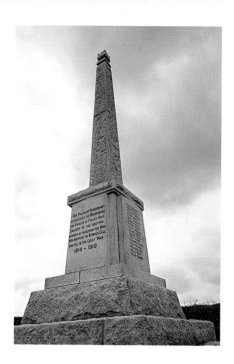

The pit closed on Good Friday, 1965. The previous year it produced quarter of a million tons of coal at a profit of £114,557.

if there had been much inter-county rivalry in the old days: the *Shell Guide* talks tantalisingly of 'prize-fights'. I stayed true to the old main road as far as Seckington, running along a ridge from which several finely pointed church spires filled the horizon. King Ethelbald was murdered by a gang of Saxon nobles at Seckington in 757. A faded police notice was still appealing for witnesses. At the next cross-roads a more recently posted sign advertised the Newton Regis Summer Fiesta. That I was two weeks too early seemed like a lucky break.

Arable fields and by-roads busy with scurrying delivery vans brought me to the outskirts of Polesworth. I crossed the West Coast Main Line railway and drove into town. The Polesworth I encountered on my canal travels always seemed a convivial little place. I remember the woman who ran the gift shop letting me into her secret theory that Shakespeare went to school here. I said: "And I bet he shared a desk with a boy called Bacon." Certainly historians acknowledge that there was a sizeable abbey here founded in the 9th century. A half-timbered gateway remains, providing picturesque access to the imposing church, beyond which you can continue across the River Anker on a fine 18th century bridge of ten arches. Such antiquities tended to mitigate Polesworth's role as a mining town. The pit closed on Good Friday, 1965. The previous year it produced quarter of a million tons of coal at a profit of £114,557. A good deal of this coal was carried by narrowboat along the canal to the electricity generating plant at Hawkesbury on the outskirts of Coventry. Some of it went as far south as the paper mills of Hertfordshire. David Blagrove wrote vividly of the loading process at Pooley Hall colliery in *Bread Upon The Waters*. Now, it goes without saying, the Coventry Canal is used for leisure only, whilst the purlieus of the mine have become a

Heritage Centre. Such makeovers usually send me scurrying for cover, scared that what post-industrial atmosphere remained, has been lost in the translation. But curiosity got the better of me, and I eased the Morgan up a metalled lane to see what they had done with the site of the colliery.

I need not have been so concerned. What I found was a car park on a wasteground of wildflowers, and a path which led down to a log cabin in the woods, from which a man emerged in friendly fashion to welcome me to the Heritage Centre. It has been built to provide an insight to the mining industry and new forms of sustainable power generation such as wind

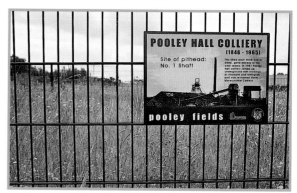

Pit head remains - Pooley Hall

and solar. A third of the site is also deemed to be of Special Scientific Interest, and there are waymarked paths around the base of the old spoil tip and past pools which were formed when floodwater from the River Anker filled areas of subsidence left over from mining days.

Thankfully, after making me feel at home, the curator wandered off to see to the needs of other visitors, and I was able to make my way around the centre unchaperoned. For what has essentially been a Community Project, I found the whole thing very well done. I sat through a screening of a video which featured interviews with old miners and their wives which I thoroughly enjoyed. One interviewee spoke of his workmates as 'smashing blokes' and I sensed that, for all the hardness and danger of work underground, the spirit of community engendered would not find its equal in present day Polesworth, more or less a 'dormitory' town now for people whose work takes them to Coventry and Tamworth and Nuneaton or even further afield. The video also taught me that Pooley pit had an incredibly fast cage in which miners were lowered to the coal seams at over six metres a second; that the management had access to their own private tennis court; and that the pithead was the first in the country to be fitted with baths where the miners could wash before going home, and that these had been ceremoniously opened by no less a dignitary than the Duke of York (later King George VI) in 1924.

Back outside again, I felt like a miner just up from underground, looking forward to getting back home to the wife and my pigeons, though not necessarily in that order. On the way back down into Polesworth I pulled up beside a potato field to pay homage to a memorial for the men of Pooley Hall Colliery who escaped the dangers of mining only to die in the Great War. Nearby, overlooking the canal, but masked largely from the road by trees, stands Pooley Hall, which dates from 1509 and which is, the last I heard, now the home of a well known soul singer. What a cornucopia of weird juxtapositions and unlikely trivia Polesworth proved to be!

Inevitably, I couldn't prize myself away from Polesworth without visiting Chester's excellent bookshop. It seems an odd, out of the way place to play host to such a good secondhand bookdealer, but the range of stock is invariably excellent, and the collection of mounted prints on sale also well worth flicking through. Twenty minutes later I came away greatly pleased by the acquisition of a pristine copy of Robert H. Goodsall's 1953 book *The Kentish Stour*: if nothing else, my journeys with a Morgan were providing me with much fresh material for my library.

The road to Dordon is paved, not so much with good intentions, let alone gold, but with 'sleeping policemen', and you know well by now my Morgan's antipathy to them. I began to feel as if I was at sea in a swell in a small boat. Tedium set in as we progressed slowly past rows of miners cottages culminating in the premises of the Dordon Working Men's Club & Institute.

Dordon is not easily visually confused with its auricular near namesake, the Dordogne.

I crossed Watling Street and exchanged Ordnance Survey maps, the old one inch sheet No.120 (Derby & Burton-upon-Trent) giving way to No.131 (Birmingham). Birmingham, I'm sure you know, used to be in Warwickshire until the local government re-organisations of 1974 landed it within the boundaries of some phoney county imaginatively known as the West Midlands. Quarter of a century is a long time to wait to extract retribution, but the publication of this book of journeys through the midland counties makes the gesture of personal protest by ignoring the existence of the West Midlands whatsoever. And in doing so I have cut my nose to spite my face, because I love Birmingham and the Black Country very much.

Beyond the A5, a by-road took me round the alluringly naked shoulder of an old colliery spoil heap. I crossed the trackbed of a former mineral railway and came to a little hamlet called Wood End. Warwickshire still has a working deep mine at Daw End near Nuneaton - the southernmost deep mine in Britain - but all the other mines in the district, such as Kingsbury, Birch Coppice, and Tame Valley are long gone, only these strange little communities of workmen's houses give any clue as to the former industrialisation of the neighbourhood. My 1947 map showed a mineral line cutting across Hurley Common, but as keen-eyed as I like to think I am in such matters, of it on the ground I could find no trace.

At Hurley itself a man was tending a vegetable patch and two neighbours chatting over a communal privet hedge: all turned to watch me and my yellow apparition go by.

"There goes Jeremy blinking Clarkson if I a'int mistaken," said neighbour No.1.

"Aye, without t'hair," replied No.2, pithily.

Fairly instinctively, it must be said, I found my way to Furnace End. Past fields of pea and potato crops I zig-zagged, breaking frequently to avoid the wholesale slaughter of moorhens, collared doves and bullfinches who seemed to regard the road as a tarmacadamed playground. I had gained height once more and could see for miles across a countryside of spires towards the sculptured ranks of the Second City. But this little corner of North Warwickshire felt just like the back of beyond. Furnace End doesn't warrant an entry in the *Shell Guide* which is a bit of an oversight on Douglas

Map reading in the pea fields

Clinker-built fishermens' boats - Shustoke Reservoir

Hickman's part, if only to note its location at the junction of the Birmingham to Leicester and Tamworth to Coventry roads and to elucidate as to the origins of its workaday name.

When my father had caught all the trout at Eyebrook he set about emptying the reservoirs at Shustoke. In this I aided and abetted him, not with a rod, but with a Grace Darling like ability to row in the face of the high waves which were often a feature of these wide expanses of water. You could tell when you were in for a rough day as soon as you let yourself into the boathouse, for the waves would slap against the hulls of the fishermens' punts with a furious sound not unlike that one might hear outside a headmaster's study when a punishment session was in full swing. Also I remember the strangely appealing smell of brackish water mixed with fish scales and oilskins - a heady cocktail, I can tell you. The boathouse was a gothic creation with an interior reminiscent of a railway waiting room. When you returned from the high seas you weighed your catch here and recorded it in the ledger for other, less adept anglers to shake their

heads at in wonderment.

I suppose I began to fear the worse when I saw that Severn Trent had provided a formal car park, and that the rim of the as yet out of view reservoir had been littered with interpretive boards. Happy families were setting off to walk their dogs and, perspiring profusely, an overweight man was returning from an abortive jog. Shustoke my Shustoke, what had become of you? For a moment I wondered hopefully if time had played a trick on me, and that I would find the little world of boyhood further round the reservoir. But it soon became all too obvious that the past had been air-brushed out of existence. The corporate Philistines had seen fit to demolish my lovely little Gothic boathouse. They just can't leave anything alone can they? And the wide waters which had been my uncharted inland ocean now had brightly-sailed dinghies racing fatuously across them like a flotilla of toy boats in the bath. By the waters of Shustoke I sat down and wept, and for a moment of unalloyed despair felt like flinging myself into the reservoir. A young ranger approached me with concern on his face, and must have found me unnecessarily truculent in tone when I asked him what had happened to the boathouse.

"It's not been here in my time," he said, pointing to the foundations, "but I think it may have been demolished ten years or so ago."

Nowadays fishing seems confined to the smaller of the two reservoirs, somewhere we would only go when the fish weren't rising in the big one. I dutifully made my way along the lane to this other reservoir, so slowly because of more 'sleeping policemen' that the Morgan grew hot and bothered and the cooling fan kept cutting in. I passed one or two employees' houses, which looked as if they dated from the time of my boathouse judging by their gothic embellishments. Not for the first time it occurred to me that the life of a reservoir keeper must be quite idyllic. A wooden hut now suffices for piscatorial records, though I was pleased to note the presence of two clinker-hulled rowing boats, rather smarter than the utilitarian punts of yore. To drown my sorrows I drove back to The Plough, the roadside inn where we would sometimes seek refreshment between sessions on the water, my father drinking beer, Vimto and Walkers Crisps for me. You can guess what I ordered.

Now my route lay due south, on by-roads to Meriden, reputedly the centre of England. At Maxstoke I came upon a ruined priory and a handsome red sandstone gateway. Some temporary looking signs pointed to a car park. I followed them into a farmyard and asked a man loitering there if the priory was open to the public?

"No, the car park's for the church bazaar," he told me, continuing: "If you want to see round the priory you must get written permission from Mrs Tie-rack."

At least that's what I think he called her, though I may have misheard above the Morgan's roar, it may well have been Mrs Sock-shop, or Mrs Knickerbox for all I know.

The Parish Council produced guide booklet to Meriden contains two colour photographs which cogently demonstrate the gulf between the rural England of the past and the quasi- ersatz rural England of the present. One depicts handcarts under an elm tree, the other kerbstones, double-yellow lines and parked cars. 'The 1958 by-pass left the quietened village prey to speculative builders', the *Shell Guide* politely puts it. Ian Nairn would have been less restrained. I stood on the green, imagining him striding across to the ugly modern shopfronts and brash new houses brandishing a metaphoric pick-axe and uttering oaths at the oafs who let this sort of thing happen. God knows how they got away with it. I suppose someone was in someone else's pocket, either financially or as a result of some sexual indiscretion or inducement.

Vimto and Walkers Crisps - The Plough Inn, Shustoke

The Blacklocks - Meriden

"I'll let you into our secret now," said Peter, as I finished photographing them against the backdrop of the obelisk. "Next month we're going to cycle across France from the Atlantic to the Mediterranean, what do you think of that?"

"Meet you in Marseille," I laughed, "apres la guerre!"

Had Meriden not been raped and pillaged by the same generic sub-species who did for Shustoke, it might still look like Berkswell. That Berkswell is beautiful, we had discovered one sunny autumn afternoon following an impromptu picnic beside the Blythe at Hampton-in-Arden. It is extraordinary how many unspoilt places one can find within a stone's throw of Birmingham if - and here's the secret - one doesn't set out to look for them. The village green still boasts stocks - I wished they still had them at Meriden for the punishment of councillors. The green also has one of those circular seats which go around the trunk of a tree. I imagine there must be some arcane term for this, an annular arboreal buttock rehabilitative perhaps. But I remember such seats with affection from village greens the length and breadth of the country: Marbury in Cheshire springs to mind, as does Ascott-under-Wychwood

I fell in with two middle-aged brothers who had propped their bicycles against a bench and begun tucking into sandwiches. They were the Blacklocks, Peter and John, and they were on their way to Arley to buy some accessories for their bicycles. I asked them if they had stopped to pay their respects to the obelisk erected in memory of the 'cyclists' who gave their lives in the two world wars, but it transpired that Meriden was just a convenient place to break their journey on their way over from Kenilworth.

"Any idea why the monument was put up here," I asked.

"There's some story that dispatch riders from the midlands used to say to each other 'meet you in Meriden after the war'," said Peter, "but don't quote me on that."

Sorry Peter, but it's such a poignant explanation, I think it's worth recording, fact or fiction. They were a jolly pair of chaps, and John proudly showed me his Raleigh, adding sadly that he had heard that the works in Nottingham was just weeks away from closure.

Porch and sundial, Berkswell Church

in Oxon. It's difficult to explain why such seats should prove more conducive to contemplation than any other public bench, but perhaps it is something to do with the fact that you can move round them as the sun moves round the bole of the tree, prolonging the state of unoccupied bliss from dawn to dusk.

Berkswell has some pretty almshouses, a well (once used for baptisms), a village shop (where I purchased an ice cream and an excellent illustrated history of the area for the very reasonable sum of £4.95) and a most handsome church, made especially notable by the provision of a half-timbered porch dating from the 16th Century. An amusing story relating to this porch concerns the habit of an 18th century parson to keep a hobby horse in its upper room because he felt he was able to give more lively sermons on horseback, all of which set me thinking that I might be well served by making my office resemble the driving controls of a South Shields trolleybus, or the wheelhouse of a Humber keel, or the footplate of a Peppercorn Pacific, in order to get the best out of my muse.

It was fast approaching the hour of noon and I needed refreshment. Glancing at the map I could see that if I got to Balsall Common I could find my way via Meer End, Honiley and Haseley Knob to Five Ways where I had long meant to visit an apparently unspoilt inn called The Case is Altered. Perennially in Camra's *Good Beer Guide*, which calls it a 'traditional, quiet, rural gem', it also features in their national inventory of heritage pubs, no mean accolade. So I drove along at a stately forty miles an hour in a state of high anticipation, salivating ever so slightly at the thought of that first cool taste of ale in my throat, the slaking of thirst, that long plunge down into the amber pool of mild intoxication.

A bloke in a Jaguar and I were the first customers. I put him down as a retired businessman. A man from the motor trade, I fancied. He had the *Daily Telegraph* tucked under his arm, and the way he made himself at home suggested that this was all part of his daily routine. He passed the time of day with the landlady, patted a spaniel called Sammy, then settled down to the crossword. I ordered a pint of Hook Norton and asked if sandwiches were available.

"I don't do any food," the landlady replied, pleasantly enough, but with a degree of intransigence, as if to say: 'this is a respectable public house, if you want namby-pamby food you can go down the road to the nearest

The Case is Altered - Five Ways

Beefeater, this is a real pub for real men, so take your pint over there and behave yourself before I set Sammy on you.

"I've got crisps," she conceded, as if suddenly noticing how my bottom lip had dropped, and fearing that I might burst into tears or, worse still, plunge my hand into my haversack and extract a Tupperware container of smoked salmon sandwiches.

"That's fine," I said with a fixed grin, "I'll have a packet of ready salted please."

Ready salted! In a pub as authentic as this, your salt should come in dark blue paper twists, ready to be applied as desired.

I found a dark corner where I would not destabilize the status quo, silently awarding her full marks for being put in my place: it is right and proper that newcomers to a pub be placed in limbo for a period of assimilation, lasting from, say, five to ten years, depending on the misanthropic tendencies of the landlord or landlady. Personally, I can't bear those pubs where they welcome you, a perfect stranger, as if you'd just come off the golf course together, following a creditable draw on the last green, only for you to catch sight of them, as soon as they've effusively served you your first pint, running madly amok in the field outside, hacking at the local farmer's innocent herd of prize Charolais bullocks with a butcher's cleaver, fawningly returning in due course with the news that: "the fatted calf is ready for you now, sir, nice and juicy and pink in the middle, just how I know you like it ."

A clock ticked, a stuffed perch in a glass case winked balefully at me, I tried to eat the crisps as silently as if I had been in a cinema. A newcomer entered and ordered a 'dizzy blonde'. The landlady received him with informal equanimity.

"Hallo Bruce," he said to the man with the Jaguar, I meant to bring you *The Mercury*, there was a special offer in it, £89 return by air to the Isle of Man."

"The figure I was given was £130," replied Bruce belligerently, suspecting he had been taken for a ride much further than the Isle of Man. There followed a lively debate on the iniquities of price hikes and mark ups, and its argumentative ripples spread out as far as the bars of Majorca, and the inflationary effect of the introduction of the Euro. I switched off, and looked at the decor, for it was indeed a beautifully unspoilt pub, even if the toilets looked anachronistically clean and up to date. Admiring a framed poster advertising the ales of Lucas, Blackwell & Arkwright, and mellowed by the Hook Norton, I fell into reflecting on the nature of pubs, and what makes a good one, and why it's such a subtle recipe that it eludes most private landlords and virtually all pub chains.

A highly subjective parade of personal favourites marched nostalgically through my mind: The Jubilee near the engine sheds in York, where I sank my first pint for the princely sum of 1/10d; the Alice Hawthorn at Nun Monkton, where the Ouse becomes the Ure; the Horsehoes at Warham in North Norfolk; the White Lion at Marsworth in Herts; the Boat Inn at Ashleworth on the banks of the Severn; the Great Western in Wolverhampton; the Shore Inn at Portsoy, near Banff. Like a list of former lovers, they had little in common, apart from an ephemeral fascination, and one might be *bitterly* disappointed if one ever attempted to go back.

Driving a Morgan along a motorway is not an exercise to be recommended to the faint of heart. It would be easier to land a bi-plane at Heathrow on Easter Friday. But you have two advantages over the towering juggernauts and family saloons that crowd you in on either side: manoeuvrability and speed. And once you have got the hang of things, nothing could be more exhilarating. Suddenly you become a prince among paupers, a winged messenger, a figure of mystery and romance overtaking the humdrum and the banal with such velocity that all of sudden you notice that all the other vehicles travelling in your direction appear to have parked up and switched off their engines.

I write metaphorically, of course, just in case the foregoing should arouse the suspicions of the Warwickshire Constabulary. But one doesn't need to break the speed limit in a Morgan to feel the wonder of flight. You are as a yachtsman to the steerer of a cabin cruiser, a steam locomotive footplateman to diesel railcar driver, a ploughman in control of two fine Suffolk Punches to the driver of a John Deere, a balloonist to a passenger in an airliner. Character is everything - considerations of comfort come a poor second.

Seven minutes after joining the M40 at Junction 15, I got off it at Junction 12. Topographically it was as akin to passing under the Channel. I emerged from the slip road into a totally different landscape, and took some convincing that I was really still in the same county. Conveniently, Upton House, my next destination, was signposted from the motorway. My dash had brought me to the southern end of Warwickshire, where it borders on Oxfordshire. The Midlands, you sense, are petering out, rolling over to have their tummy tickled by the Home Counties. From the National Trust Handbook I had gleaned that Upton House had belonged to the Chairman of Shell, and that it contained an exhibition of that company's publicity material. And seeing as how the *Shell Guides* had been frequently consulted vade-mecums on my journeys through the Midland Shires, I thought it would be an appropriate property to visit.

The signposted route took me up to the escarpment of Edge Hill. A steep ascent through the woods on the B4086 ensued, before I turned right, running along the top of the ridge. I came upon an interesting pub called The Castle, topped by a quaint tower. Northwards the view extended for miles into a misty distance, the site of the opening battle of the Civil War in 1642. At the end of this road I took a left on to the A422 before encountering the entrance gates to Upton House.

Upton was left to the National Trust in 1948 by the 2nd Viscount Bearsted, the son of the man who had founded the great oil company, Shell. The house itself has earlier origins, but was extensively remodelled by Walter Samuel (aka the 2nd Viscount) following his purchase of the property

The driveway - Upton House

Upton House
Top left: The exterior, looking south
Lower left: The swimming pool, looking west
Below: The swimming pool, detail

136

in 1927. Samuel was an art collector of some substance - not surprisingly with the wealth of Shell behind his purchasing power - and the house contains a ravishing collection of paintings and porcelain. I joined a sizeable crowd of visitors in a perambulation of the interior of the house. Blithely I came upon paintings by Stubbs, Constable, El Greco, Turner, and Brueghel and tried to empathise with the excitement a collector must have experienced in acquiring them. But it was not until I came upon two upper floor rooms given over to the advertising of Shell's petroleum products that my own passions were aroused.

In common with the railway companies in the first half of the 20th century, Shell understood that subliminal advertising was the most effective means of increasing trade. After all, petrol was invisible, so it could hardly be advertised directly. The trick - as the railways also realised - was to make people want to travel, and in travelling to use Shell petrol. And in common with the railways, Shell set about encouraging travel in two distinct ways: by publishing guide books to encourage the Great British public to explore their country, and by commissioning first class artists to create lively posters with which to capture the public eye. The guide books, several samples of which were on display in glass cases, kicked off with a volume covering *Cornwall* in 1934, compiled by no less an authority on architecture and landscape than John Betjeman. Within a year *Kent*, *Derbyshire* and *Wiltshire* were added before the responsibility for publishing passed from the Architectural Press to B. T. Batsford. In 1938 John Piper's *Oxfordshire* was published and he shared editorship with Betjeman until the latter's resignation in 1967, thereafter taking sole charge until the last guide, covering *Nottinghamshire*, was published by Faber & Faber in 1984. Faber & Faber had taken over the publishing rights just before the Second World War.

In retrospect the series, viewed as an entity, appears coherent enough - though there are glaring gaps in the coverage of important counties like Yorkshire, Lancashire and Cheshire - but by all accounts the relationship between Shell and the various publishers, and Betjeman in particular, wasn't always harmonious. Much evidence suggests that the series was not commercially successful. Shell's financial input obviously helped to underwrite production costs, but subsequent sales often failed to financially reflect the time and effort put in. The guides to some counties hardly sold a thousand copies over several years. Another problem concerned editorial integrity. At a late stage Shell's marketing executives would often intervene

with requests for certain gazetteer entries to be toned down. In 1960 David Verey's *Mid-Wales* guide raised an outcry in Llandindrod Wells which had been portrayed (probably with reason) as a place of incessant rain, and the inhabitants threatened to boycott Shell products. James Lees-Milne's *Worcestershire* and Juliet Smith's *Northamptonshire* also called for the 'blue pencil' treatment, and whereas Shell's blushes may have been spared, the editors and the writers must have been sorely disillusioned. Right from the outset, Betjeman had wanted the guides to be 'critical' in their approach, yet I know from personal experience just how brittle, not to say blinkered, parochial and municipal pride can be. Ironically, the entries in the Gazetteer of some *Shell Guides* can sometimes be quite dry, but the black & white photography is rarely less than inspirational, and when the shortlived *New Shell Guides* briefly made an appearance in the 1980s with colour photography, something of the magic of the series was missing.

I had hitherto considered my own collection of *Shell Guides* reasonably impressive, but now my mouth was watering over a selection of first editions with spiral binding and Bauhaus typography and graphics the like of which I had not set eyes on before: *Northumberland & Durham* in one volume by Thomas Sharp; *Buckinghamshire* by John Nash; *Hampshire* by John Rayner, *The West Coast of Scotland* by Stephen Bone. Later editions now commonly cost £25 or more in secondhand bookshops, but these earlier samples must be worth hundreds. As far as I am concerned, however, the *Shell Guides* are not merely collectibles. When I first began compiling guide books to the canals in 1980 they quickly became a source of reference, but more importantly, of inspiration. My sorrow is that the places they portrayed so innocently and timelessly in black & white are all too often now ugly, over-coloured, car-filled caricatures of their former selves.

Shell posters were originally displayed on boards carried on the sides or rear of delivery lorries. They bore slogans such as 'See Britain First on Shell' or 'Everywhere You Go You Can Be Sure Of Shell' and 'These Men Use Shell', and the often stunningly beautiful imagery of the artwork was capable of melting even the stoniest stay-at-home heart. Artists of considerable reputation and calibre were recruited to execute these works: Rex Whistler, Graham Sutherland, Paul Nash, Lord Berners, Tom Purvis, John Piper, Vanessa Bell. Of the posters on exhibit, I was particularly drawn to Tom Purvis's *How To Buy Oil*, which featured a yellow open seater not unlike the one at that moment residing in the car park; Vanessa Bell's pointillistic approach to Alfriston in Sussex; Richard Guyatt's *Racing Motorists*; and Paul Nash's *Footballers Prefer Shell*. Also, of local significance to me, was *'Roman' Tower, Tutbury* by L. H. Rosoman, largely because the subject matter stands less than five miles away from where I live. I can only urge you to go and see for yourself the beauty and adventure of this artwork. It's a knack we've lost. Advertising in the 21st century is good at humour and irony, but aesthetics trail behind, as if the appreciation of form and colour were a weakness to be mocked.

Before we go out into the grounds there is just one room I must point out to you - the bathroom! It was created for Dorothy Samuel in Art Deco style by the architect Percy Morley Horder soon after the property had been purchased in 1927. It was designed to compliment the adjoining master bedroom where the theme was Chinese. Walter Samuel had inherited his father Marcus's love of all things eastern. Marcus Samuel had originally built his business empire trading in exotic shells from the Far East, hence the name given to the petroleum company in due course. Anyway, I digress! Dorothy's bathroom was equipped with a shower and a bidet and a huge built-in bath all painted in red, black and silver - even the vaulted ceiling was lacquered in aluminium leaf. The result is oddly masculine for a woman's bathroom (Walter Samuel effected his ablutions in much smaller premises!) more like a Chinese Laundry than a domestic bathroom, but there is no getting away from its impact. Sadly, visitors to Upton House, are not issued with bathing coupons.

Outside the skies had darkened and a light drizzle was falling. The fecund aroma of wet earth rose up from the flower beds. I wandered around the grounds experiencing that not readily quenchable sadness that comes with the realization that one will never ever amass the sort of wealth required to sustain life in such surroundings. But it was not only sorrow for myself I felt, but a lament for Walter and Dorothy Bearsted that the gorgeous world they had created for themselves was now open to the *hoi polloi*, the likes of me and you and our insatiable curiosity for how the other half live.

Those gardens, though, they are achingly lovely, layers of terraces plunging down steeply to a lake thick with reeds and lilies. In one corner of the main lawn, discreetly to the side of the house, I came upon an outdoor swimming pool. It was like something out of a Hockney painting, even under grey skies. It called out for a photograph, so I put my bag down and set about arriving at a suitable exposure, careful also to keep my lens out of the rain. I must have had my back to her, for there was a sudden splash and, as I looked around in surprise, a woman's head burst to the surface in an explosion of pewter coloured droplets. She proceeded to swim the length of the pool with easy, graceful strokes. The smile on her face didn't seem focused on me. As she approached my end of the pool I gestured an apology for the intrusion, but she ignored this and executed an immaculate turn. Astonished, I watched her swim away from me, noticing for the first time the palest of pink satin robes flung casually over the back of the diving board. It was presumptuous of me, I know, but I couldn't help pressing the shutter release at her disappearing form. Then, shamefaced, I scurried away into the trees as a man's voice called from the house: "Dorothy, Dorothy, are you in the pool?"

The sun punched its way through the cloud cover as I headed down the drive, creating that incandescent kind of light which comes only in the wake of rain. I missed the turn at Edgehill, and providentially found myself in Ratley. Providentially because it was the most beautiful of 'Cotswold' villages, slung out on a slope facing the Sor Brook, a tributary of the Cherwell which forms the boundary between Warwickshire and Oxfordshire. The lovely light gilded the ironstone buildings in a manner which made them gleam like gold. The church went by the unusual name of St Peter & Vincula, but I was more taken with a Nonconformist chapel perched half-way up the precipitous main street. Had it been later in the afternoon, I might have called it a day, and sought supper at the Rose & Crown, which was highly thought of by the *Good Beer Guide*. Instead, I conscientiously put my foot down and roared up the hill out of the village before I was seduced into staying put for eternity.

The remnants of an old railway caught my eye as I turned off the B4086 and dropped down into Arlescote. Give me my due. I have not bored you stiff with the A-Z of every railway line encountered on these journeys. I have stayed stiff-lipped. Aching alone for lines long lost. So humour me now. Please let me tell you that what I saw were the remains of the Edge Hill Light Railway, an extremely short-lived branch off the Stratford & Midland Junction Railway opened in 1920 to carry iron ore out of the neighbouring hills. And guess who engineered it? Why that's right, the Colonel himself, H. F. Stephens, and for his trouble he was issued with a

Reading Room - Avon Dassett

Old Tower - Burton Dassett

free pass for travel anywhere on the SMJ. One hopes he made good use of it, the EHLR closed within five years!

Arlescote was followed by Avon Dassett. I was beginning to get a tad blasé in my response to the beauty of all these 'Cotswold' villages, with their organic commitment to the earth. But the *Shell Guide* waxed lyrically over the glories of the Victorian Gothic Revival church of 1868, while my own attention was drawn to the survival of a Reading Room in the village; how very civilised and commendable.

I turned left towards the Country Park at Burton Dassett. Usually 'Country Park's sound all a bit too municipal for my liking. They smack of organised games and community singing and seeking to arrange the gender of your child prior to conception. But give it its due, Burton Dassett Country Park has a series of panoramic views to die for, and the sort of thymy turf heaven-made for flinging oneself down upon on hot, still days in order to complete that elusive last stanza of your latest poem while the larks sing merrily above.

From the toposcope, six hundred feet and a bit above sea level, you can see for miles. The Malverns rise up to the west, forty miles away; the Clee Hills, just to the left of Birmingham, fifty-two miles away. It's the perfect place for hill-spotters. Unfortunately, on this occasion, the weather wasn't up to lying spread-eagle on the grass. Heavy, ink black rain clouds were billowing over from the Malvern Hills. From the top of Beacon Hill I watched their sullen approach like a fleet of landing craft bearing an invading army. I calculated that I had about eight minutes before the heavens opened. Just long enough to rig up my tripod and set a timed exposure. Long enough, that is, if the wind hadn't wanted to join in, playfully blowing the tripod over every time I set off to run to the top of the hill. I got back to the car just as the first machine-gun hail rattled on the roof.

Tired by my exertions in the hills, I began to think longingly of supper, picturing a corner table in a convivial inn, some warm comfort food and a companionable glass of ale. I dropped down through Fenny Compton, noticing that the local stone was more mellow in colour than in those villages behind me. Crossing the Oxford Canal, I climbed to Wormleighton, a narcotic, depopulated village of weatherbeaten stone with a 17th century gatehouse, before proceeding to Priors Hardwick, where the Butchers Arms

Old Gatehouse, Wormleighton

advertised Anglo-Portugese cooking and appeared, its stonework shyly peeping from behind bountiful hanging baskets, to be just what the doctor ordered. I parked and went to the door. It was locked, no one responded to my polite tap, and I could hear no reassuring movement within. It was disappointing, but it was not the end of the world. Priors Marston lay just down the road and there was bound to be a pub there.

But first I drove to Marston Doles, where the nine locks of the Napton flight deliver the Oxford Canal safely into the arms of its summit. I have always had a soft spot for the unusual, trapezium-shaped warehouse which stands alongside the sharp bend in the canal beyond the top lock. It has been converted into offices, and the transformation has rid it of some of its old, brooding character, but it's still worth a detour to see. The eleven, dizzy, dreamy miles of the summit could be accomplished in less than half the distance by a single-minded crow, and as I wrote in my *Oxford & Grand Union Canal Companion* 'with a compass, a pair of stout walking shoes and a healthy disregard for the laws of trespass, you could do it in four'.

But no boater or towpath-walker in their right minds would begrudge the extra distance involved, and there are times in the canal's convoluted traverse of these remote farmlands when the appearance of another boat on what seems to be an entirely different canal is just an optical illusion.

The pub in Priors Marston - I have blanked its name from my memory - was closed. 'They drink late in this part of the world' I mused as I drove on to Napton. Napton-on-the-Hill is a charming village laid out upon the slopes of a south-facing hill and topped by a windmill with sails. Because of its locks, its hire bases and its proximity to an important junction with the Grand Union Canal, it is a pivotal point on the inland waterways network. Consequently no less than four pubs remain open in the village, catering for the chronic thirst of those who would work locks and those who would watch them. With four pubs to choose from I chose one which provided me with one of the most dire and inedible bar meals I have ever had the misfortune to encounter. The laws of libel deter me from giving any clues as to the identity of this establishment. Suffice it to say they will not be gracing the next edition of my canal guide, not, that is, without a change of chef, if chef indeed there was.

So that was the damp squib which ended a partially damp day in Warwickshire. Driving home I wasn't sure if the bad taste in my mouth was down to that appalling meal, or a little nagging fear that I hadn't, after all my heart searching and map reading, seen the best of this elusive county. And yet tucked up in bed that night, flipping through Douglas Hickman's *Shell Guide to Warwickshire*, I sensed that the county had tricked him too, keeping something back, like a shy person who comes over merely as sullen. One day I'll go back and meet Warwickshire, half way ...

Running Uphill - Burton Dassett

Wheatfield & Malverns

Broadway at my back, I bowled down into the Vale of Evesham like a
child rolling down a hill, delightfully giddy by the time I got to the bottom,
and hoping my day out in Worcestershire would be as fruitful as the county
itself. It is difficult to disguise an ending, whether it be the
ending of a journey, or a football match, or a relationship,
or a life, or, as in this case, a book. The reader realises
that there are only so many pages left and that some
sort of line is about to be drawn. Thus I was in a
frame of mind to make the most of my final county,
before the day to day demands of work and home
and Middle age brought me back to earth with a bump.

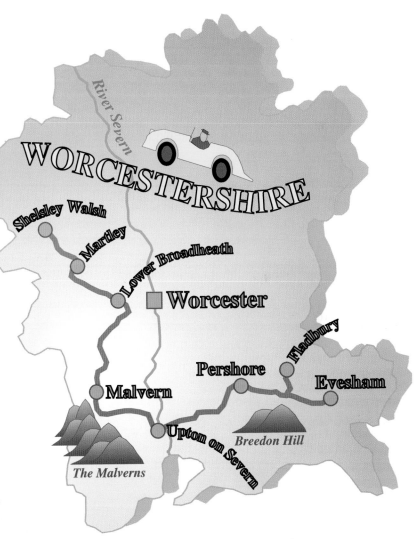

What a wonderful county Worcestershire is, small but perfectly formed,
and watered by some beautiful rivers. I have journeyed on its inland
waterways and travelled by its trains, and I can't remember it ever letting
me down. I am glad that it seems to have divorced itself from Herefordshire.
When the meddling Government re-organisations of 1974 merged them
together, it was like seeing two people you're very fond of getting married
for the wrong reason.

It took me twenty minutes to get through Bengeworth from the Ring
Road, Bengeworth being to Evesham as Pest is to Buda, the poorer relation
on the wrong side of the river. The river in question being the Avon of
course, 'Shakespeare's Avon' as it's commonly known, though you have
to look hard and long through his plays and poems to find any mention
of the name. I left the Morgan muttering in a multistorey and emerged
from a side door into the green open swards of Abbey Park, being treated
to the sonorous chimes of ten o'clock from the carillon in the Bell Tower,
the sole surviving remnant of an abbey demolished after the Dissolution.
Ten of the clock also marked the opening of the door at The Almonry, an

143

"Run your eye down an old map of the Avon and you'll see the inscription 'ferry' at fairly frequent intervals. Here, lean over my shoulder, we'll look together: Offenham, Hampton, Chadbury, Fladbury, Wyre Piddle."

ancient half timbered house which hosts the Heritage and Tourist Information centres. Armed with a sheaf of leaflets, I emerged to do Evesham justice, but got waylaid by a sign pointing to 'Hampton Ferry'. That ferries (not flattery) will get you everywhere, is an old Pearson aphorism. It must spring from childhood renditions of the negro spiritual *Michael Row the Boat Ashore*. 'Hallelujah,' I thought, as I walked down the lane to the ferry, past the Interflora man delivering a bouquet of lilies to No.2. A man in a Vauxhall Corsa wound down his window as I approached.

"Excuse me," he said, "do you know if there's a car boot sale on down there?"

"I can't say," I replied, "but the one you've got looks perfectly roomy". His wife tittered, before the window went up, impressively quickly.

'In the unlikely event of the general public ever purchasing our guide books in sufficient quantities to enable us to retire, we would buy out the ferry rights on some remote reach of some lazily winding river - preferably with a water mill attached - and settle down contentedly for the rest of our lives'. That small extract from *Pearson's Railway Rides - Cotswolds & Malverns* succinctly sums up my

devotion to inland ferries. Sadly, neither that, nor yet any other book of mine, has made my fortune. I plod on, hacking my way through the literary undergrowth, a profit with plenty of loss in his own land.

Run your eye down an old map of the Avon and you'll see the inscription 'ferry' at fairly frequent intervals. Here, lean over my shoulder, we'll look together: Offenham, Hampton, Chadbury, Fladbury, Wyre Piddle. Only Hampton remains in use, flourishing as a short cut for shoppers, caravan dwellers and the occasional rambler. Disguised as the latter, I strolled down to the riverbank and found the ferryman in his punt waiting Micawberishly for trade to turn up. The operation is simplicity defined. A chain stretches from bank to bank. When boats wish to pass the chain is submerged. At other times it hangs perhaps three feet above the water and the ferryman hauls you over, hand over hand. The whole transaction takes barely a minute and there is scant time for small talk. Fifty pence changes hands and you savour the moment. What, after all, is the done thing? Is one expected to pass the time of day with Sharon as he rows you over the Styx? We will all find out in due course, all I can suggest is that you get yourself down to Hampton for a practice run. And a Desert Island list of ferries? Scotland is comparatively rich in them yet, and I have enjoyably sampled Nigg, Camusnagaul, and Castle Threave in recent years. In England I would draw your attention to the lower reaches of the Tyne, the Manchester Ship Canal, Walberswick, Hampton Loade, Normanton-on-Soar and Pile Island. Of Wales I have no cognizance at all, save for Fairbourne to Barmouth.

After the idyll, incongruity: I had to negotiate a labyrinth of static homes in order to find my way back into Evesham via the Abbey Bridge. Eventually, much to the chagrin of the Minotaur, I reached the A44 and walked down the hill past St Andrews, the parish church of Great & Little Hampton. Two old dears were hovering outside the lych gate: "I'm waiting for Gwen, we're going to clean the brasses." Did they grow up in the realization that one day St Andrew's

HAMPTON FERRY · EVESHAM

FARES

Adults 50. EACH WAY.
Children 25. EACH WAY.

Scenes at Hampton Ferry

Gilded tomb, St Andrews, Hampton

Sculler & Swans, Evesham

brasses would be the fulcrum of their lives? Presently I returned to the banks of the Avon, albeit hidden from view behind a hedge of convolvulus. Abbey Bridge is built of concrete on the bow span principal. It was a less romantic way to cross the river than the Hampton Ferry, but at least I was treated to the sight of a young female rower sculling effortlessly by below. She was rowing a single scull and took me back to schooldays on the Yorkshire Ouse. In similar slender craft I ranged from Poppleton in the north to Naburn in the south, glad to escape when the opportunity arose, from the hearty gregariousness and team spirit of 'the eight'. So much rather would I have preferred sculling up and down river on my own, I had the temerity to ask the rowing master if he would let me swap places with a boy not as yet selected for the crew, though very much hoping to be so. Such an outrageous demand met with the response it deserved: "Pearson, I pick the crew, not you - go away!"

Under Bredon Hill I drove along the A44 as far as Cropthorne, entering a landscape which has inspired several writers who all, in turn, have inspired

me. Quiller-Couch, Francis Brett Young, Temple Thurston have all employed this corner of the Vale of Evesham as settings for novels. In modern literary values they're all has-beens and throwbacks of course, but that doesn't dilute the quality of their prose.

The Jubilee Bridge at Cropthorne carries you over the Avon into Fladbury near the site of the last water-gate on the river, a water-gate being a device for altering water levels for boat traffic without affecting the supply to mills. *The Idyllic Avon*, an effusive account of a journey upstream by rowing boat from Tewkesbury to Stratford, written by John Henry Garrett in 1906, includes a sepia photograph of a pleasure steamer waiting to pass through the Cropthorne water-gate. Those were the days; between the wars the navigation fell into disrepair, and it was not until 1962 that it became navigable again as far as Evesham, by which time conventional locks had been introduced. The river provided power for two mills in Fladbury, for a while one of them belonged to the Fladbury Electric Light Power Company who charged ten shillings per light per annum to householders in the village.

I know all this stuff because it's my job to know it. Writing guide books

means years and years of research in reference libraries, ferreting out trivia for the entertainment of an insatiable public. In consequence I am a walking encyclopaedia of useless facts, though useless at Quiz Nights because my subject range is too esoteric and arcane for the compilers to consider.

"In what year was the Fladbury Flood Bank erected?"

"1881."

"What was the name of the long-serving Fladbury ferrywoman?"

"Mrs Izod."

"How many Fladbury men served in the Great War?"

"One hundred and thirty-two."

"Which novelist lived at Craycombe House from 1932 to 1945?"

"Francis Brett Young."

"Name two items regularly despatched from Fladbury by goods train in the past."

"Plums and cabbages."

"How sad are you?"

"Pass ..."

Perhaps not unnaturally, in a village as pretty as Fladbury, the emphasis is on privacy, and access to the riverbank denied the general public, even those driving yellow Morgans. Cropthorne Mill is now in domestic use and the ferry in private hands. All I could do was gaze wistfully across at it and wish that it was 1910 and that I was Ernest Temple Thurston, a popular romantic novelist seeking local colour for a travel book I was working on called *The Flower of Gloster*, and calling over the water for the ferry to come and collect me. Instead I was being eyed suspiciously by two anglers on the mill

Pershore - the Medieval bridge over the Avon

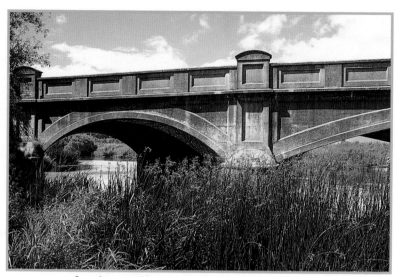

Pershore - the concrete bridge over the Avon

island in that peculiar dog-like way the English have of warding off strangers at their gates. Temple Thurston was very taken with the Avon, and used Nafford Mill, further downstream on the way to Tewkesbury, as the setting for his Richard Furlong trilogy.

Twenty odd years later another romantic novelist came to live in Fladbury. Romantic, not in a Mills & Boon sense, but in the fact that he enjoyed a wide female readership. We came across Francis Brett Young at the end of the first chapter, and it is safe to say that much of *Mr Lucton's Freedom* was written in Fladbury, at Craycombe House, a gracious 18th century property up on the neighbouring hillside. It had been built for George Perrott, one time owner of the Lower Avon Navigation, and wealthy from the success of the best-selling *Mr & Mrs Pennington*, Brett Young set about having the house restored to its former glory. He lived here with his adoring and over-protective wife, Jessie, until his ill health made them move to South Africa at the end of the Second World War. He died there in 1954, but his ashes were brought over to be interred in Worcester Cathedral. Now he is a forgotten figure, though a small but vigorous society champion his works.

There are two bridges across the Avon at Pershore - a 15th century stone bridge and a 20th century concrete bridge - prizes are not awarded for guessing correctly which has the most aesthetic appeal. On June 5th, 1644, in fleeing to Worcester after the abortive siege of Oxford, King Charles, closely persued by the Parliamentarians, ordered the stone built bridge to be demolished behind him. Unfortunately his troops took this rather too literally and some forty of them were drowned in the proceedings. Of course it was repaired after the Civil War - as all bridges are after the military men have played their little games with them - and if you look closely you can see where the stonework around the central arch differs from the rest in texture and colour. It remained the way to get across the river at Pershore until 1926, when the demands of increased motor traffic were realised in the shape of a new bridge. It was, they boasted, the first concrete bridge in the county. Their pride seems misplaced now.

I sat on the balcony of Whistlers Restaurant feeling faintly colonial and *en fete*. Below, in the wide expanse of Broad Street, the Morgan stood parked contentedly, whilst Pershore Abbey loomed over the higgledy-piggledy rooftops like a psalm transmuted into stone. Sipping Lavazza coffee and flipping through *The Times*, I savoured the passing scene, watching buses

Broad Street - Pershore

arrive and depart in quick succession, carrying those too young or too old, or too poor, or too environmentally-conscientious to make use of the motor car to facilitate their shopping. The panini I had ordered was some time in coming. I had regressed from the sports pages, to the Court Circular and Forthcoming Marriages, mischievously transposing weddings, so that Mr T. A. W. Riley-Smith would walk down the aisle with Miss F. E. C. Sawrey-Cookson, letting it be known that henceforth they would go under the quadruple-barrelled surname of Riley-Smith-Sawrey-Cookson. I also read of a Memorial Service to my former railway favourite, Sir Peter Parker, the British Rail Chairman from 1976-83. I always felt that he had the railway network's integrity at heart, which is more than can be said of many of its post war chairmen. I shook hands with him once at an award ceremony given in the wake of a poster design competition. My poster (bronze award) depicted the Advanced Passenger Train (the one which wouldn't tilt properly) running through the northern fells (Jackie painted the trees) beneath a slogan which celebrated the relaxing nature of rail travel, and how Glasgow was only an enjoyable book, a snooze and a good meal away from London by train. Embarrassingly, in hindsight, I added a bottle of Liebfraumilch, and when Sir Peter asked me 'Why Liebfraumilch?' I could only stammer 'because it's a good vintage'. How callow can you get?

Pershore Abbey

Sir Peter had Blake and MacNiece read at his memorial service, but I was thinking of John Betjeman and his poem Pershore Station, which speaks of evensong at the abbey and gas light on frosty evergreens, the evergreens, I recognised, that no Great Western station ever seemed to be without. From poetry and trains, my mind wandered to motor cars and how Pershore's picturesque streets were filled with designs of vehicle diametrically opposed to the prevalent styles of architecture. I can write with a clear, objective conscience that only my Morgan did not rankle with the scene below me, and I would go so far as to claim that no road vehicle designed since 1960 would, en masse, present a palatable, coherent aspect in any traditional English town. I am no expert, I cannot tell you why this should be so, but I am prepared to stand up and argue the point indefinitely: it is true, it is true, it is true.

My panini was delicious, but as I devoured the last tasty morsel the rain came. I hurried to pay the bill, for I had not erected the hood before I left, and the seats would be soaked. Rushing downstairs, my eye was caught by a cookery shop. I ran in, scattering sundry housewives in my wake. Barging my way to the counter, I begged them to sell me the largest tea towel they had in stock, flung the money down and raced back to the Morgan.

"Much longer," it said laconically, "and you could have converted me into a jacuzzi."

"You lack the bubbly personality," I responded, busily wiping the seats as one would a wet dog.

Hood erected and honour restored, on both sides, I made for the Abbey, and when I got there, the sun was coming out again, demonstrating how transient all our troubles might be if we only chose to treat them with the contempt they deserve. I cannot honestly remember an ecclesiastical building which has moved me more; and this in a summer when, beyond the confines of this book, I had been in the cathedrals of Amiens and Rouen. It out Fotheringhayed Fotheringhay - of which it reminded me because of its size and truncated nature - and my only disappointment was that a poster in the South Transept bore the inscription: 'No Tower Tours Today'. I envied the campanologists their lofty, vertigo-inducing platform reached via a spiral staircase and nicknamed 'the cage'. It is said to be unique and was erected by Gilbert Scott in 1864. Betjeman's poem talks of the sound of Pershore Abbey's bells 'pouring through the apple boughs for seven centuries'. A carillon rings out at 9am, noon, 3pm, 6pm and 9pm; each day, over a fortnightly cycle, playing a different tune. Every other Saturday you can hear *The Blue Bells of Scotland*! I left through the Vestry. By the exit door there's a lost property box. It bore evidence of much absent-mindedness: gloves, scarves, spectacle cases, umbrellas and, for all I knew, lost souls as well.

I left Pershore on the Upton road at a quarter to one. I hadn't gone half a mile before I was drenched.

"Now you know what it's like," guffawed the Morgan.

By Pershore Cemetery I leapt out of the car and hastily attempted to erect the hood. Fifty seconds had been my previous best, but in the fumbling panic that followed I lost all presence of mind and took much longer. Long enough, in fact, to become so wet that I almost flung the hood into the cemetery in disgust. My all round ineffectuality was further emphasised as, once underway again, the first oncoming vehicle encountered was a vintage open tourer whose insouciantly oilskin clad driver waved cheerfully to mark our brief ignominious encounter.

I climbed out of the Avon Valley, crossed the M5 motorway, and began the descent to the River Severn and Upton. The rain had passed, Upton glistened like a dog fresh from a swim. I stood back as it shook itself. 'A delightful town, redolent of river ghosts' is how Upton is described in *Pearson's Severn & Avon Companion*. The old church tower looks like a lighthouse and lends seafaring atmosphere to the scene. Once upon a time the road bridge swung. Now what swinging they do in Upton relies on the contribution of 'tribute band' concerts at the Memorial Hall. Apparently, Cher, Neil Diamond and Tina Turner were all booked to appear in the not too distant future.

I would have preferred, I know, the Upton-on-Severn that L. T. C. Rolt wrote about in his 1949 volume *Worcestershire* in the Robert Hale County Book series. In those days the river still worked for its living. Fleets of petrol barges chugged upstream to Worcester and Stourport, steam powered tugs hauled 'trains' of narrowboats, many of them loaded with chocolate ingredients destined for Cadburys at Bournville. Cadbury's made considerable use of water transport. Various raw ingredients, such as cocoa beans and sugar, would be transhipped from sea-going vessels at Gloucester docks and carried via the river and the Worcester & Birmingham Canal to Bournville.

After moulding into square cakes of chocolate 'mass' it was then returned by boat to Frampton-on-Severn, below Gloucester, for further processing before once again going back to Bournville for completion. All that barging about, no wonder it used to taste better.

Driving west under clearing skies, the Malverns looked lovely and beguiling. I'd jettisoned the hood again and chosen the B road through Hanley Swan in preference to the A road via Little Malvern. Steam rose off the seats as the increasingly warm sun burned off the damp. I might have been on some vast Romanian plain, approaching the Carpathian Mountains. At Malvern Wells I joined the main road and began skirting the escarpment, feeling like a dentist rubbing his forefinger over a patient's gums. It's a road I know well, though one I never tire of. Dropping down into Great Malvern you always half expect to see the sea, or at least some huge alpine lake, lapping at its edges, an illusion which owes its distortion in no little way to the flamboyant, resort-like architecture of the town. Retired military men, home from the far bastions of empire would often select Malvern as a place to fight their last, unwinnable battle.

On home turf, so to speak, the Morgan was in its element. Less than a mile from where it was conceived - constructed being too utilitarian a verb for a motor car of such character and personality - I could tell it felt at home. It seemed odd to be travelling through. I felt a bit irresponsible and anti-social, in case the done thing was to call in and say hello. But I didn't linger in Malvern Link. Instead I took the by-road, past The Swan at Newland, which leads across the railway to Leigh Sinton, and found my way on to the A4103. It had become a warm and beautiful afternoon, though in the distance black clouds suggested heavy showers. But in the Morgan, with the hood down, you felt like a fighter pilot, knowing, inevitably, that the enemy was out there, but being confident that you could take avoiding action when necessary, even if it meant leaving the rain just half a mile down the road. In the rear view mirror I caught glimpses of The Malverns reared up behind me, and reversed into a field of wheat to take a photograph. Then I crossed the River Teme and headed for Lower Broadheath where, I imagine you know, Edward Elgar was born.

Considering that classical music was something I grew up with, I

came upon Elgar comparatively late. Just after leaving school I bought a recording of Barbirolli conducting the *First Symphony*. If memory isn't playing tricks on me I purchased this from the HMV shop in Birmingham on the same day that I acquired a copy of L. T. C. Rolt's *Narrow Boat* from Hudson's nearby bookshop. Thus the two are inextricably linked, the music providing a sympathetic and highly appropriate soundtrack to the book; both being imbued with melancholy and Englishness in equal measure. Subsequently, a good deal of Elgar's recorded catalogue found its way into my record collection: the symphonies, the violin and cello concerti, *Enigma Variations*, *Cockaigne*, *Sea Pictures*, *In the South*, all five *Pomp & Circumstance* marches, some chamber works, sundry orchestral works, but not *The Dream of Gerontius*, because its rampant Catholicism comes too close for comfort for a misaligned 'convent boy'.

Elgar's Birthplace Museum had hitherto fallen into the 'always meaning to go to, but never got around to it' category. Had it been Arnold Bax's birthplace, or Jack Moeran's or Gerald Finzi's, nothing would have got in my way, but much as I enjoy and revere Elgar's music, and much as I admire the man, he is too famous and too popular to be deserving of my hero-worship. I am rather surprised that Edward Elgar never got around to owning a Morgan. Knowing his fascination for all things mechanical, and bearing in mind that the characterful early three-wheelers were being built on his doorstep, why didn't the two connect? Perhaps it was one craze too many for a man in his fifties by the time Morgan became an established marque. Goodness knows he had enough interests outside music: golf, horse racing, chemistry, dogs, cycling. Maybe he had a cyclist's mistrust of motoring and motorists - the two passions are often mutually exclusive because they both perceive themselves as 'kings of the road'.

But that Elgarian's can aspire to an admiration of cars was vouchsafed me as I drew into the car park under the appreciative gaze of another visitor.

"A fine car you have there," he exclaimed as I turned off the ignition.

"It's not a bad old thing," I replied, easing myself out of the

Elgar's Birthplace, Lower Broadheath

driver's seat.

"What power does she pack?"

"Three point nine litre, hundred and ninety brake horsepower, from a Rover V8," said I, deliberately not being drawn into reference to the car in terms of gender.

"And what'll she do?" he oozed oilily.

"What she's told," I remarked, regretting immediately being inveigled into his 'man to man' repartee.

"I bet," he chortled, "a bit of a goer, eh?"

Shades of *Cars & Girls* by Prefab Sprout without the irony, shades of Springsteen's *Racing in the Street* with no irony at all, just a deep and febrile love of cars.

Amidst controversy, the Elgar Foundation opened a brand new spanking Centre in 2000. Traditionalists feared that the privacy of the composer's birthplace might be compromised. Certainly the new building is out of sympathy with the neighbouring cottage, but it enables increased amounts of material to be put on display, and merchandising and retailing opportunities to be provided, that would have been inappropriate activities in the sanctity of the birthplace itself. Personally, I was more disappointed at the lack of a cafe, for I had been picturing quadrants of cake and a pot of steaming tea for some miles.

"They might be doing tea at The Plough", offered the man in reception in a jaunty manner.

"Or there's a garden centre down the road," chipped in a middle aged lady.

But what I had envisaged was a discreet tea room, with Elgar extracts being played by a real live trio, and the need for difficult decisions to be made concerning the competing merits of coffee cake or lemon sponge.

Formalities completed, I made my way out through the back door of the Elgar Centre and down through the rose-scented garden to the Birthplace Museum, the charming little brick house ('a tiny artisan's cottage of no pretensions' according to Lees-Milne) in which Edward Elgar was born in 1857. He did not live in it for very long - within a couple of years the family had moved to Worcester - but it held a position of affection in Elgar's heart, which caused him to request that his daughter Carice create a museum in his memory here. An attendant checked my ticket and languidly looked me over, judging me, I felt, to fall into the daytripper as opposed to earnest Elgar scholar category. I did nothing to disabuse him of his prejudices.

I stood in the room where he was born - punningly known as the Nursery Suite - and marvelled at the moment of a genius's arrival into the world, but, as usual with me, it was the little details which fascinated: a poster for a concert at Alcester Corn Exchange on 11th May 1881 at which Mr E. W. Elgar would play 1st violin, Mr W. H. Elgar 2nd violin and Mr H. Elgar viola; his golf clubs, a race card, his microscope; journal jottings concerning the sighting of a crocodile on the banks of the Amazon on 7th December 1923; memorabilia from other holidays spent in Italy and Germany. Such energy, I reflected, put me to shame.

Confirming the attendant's worst fears, I didn't linger long in the museum. On my way out he was deep in considered conversation with a fresh visitor over the merits of Barbirolli versus Boult as interpreters of Elgar's symphonies. I narrowly refrained from interrupting with the cheeky observation that Beecham had my vote, Beecham being notoriously, and very likely enviously, immune to the charm of Elgar's music, and on record as likening it to the musical equivalent of St Pancras station; a rather boomeranged barb, I would have thought. Back in the Elgar Centre, I perused the racks of CDs for a suitable souvenir. Selecting a recording of the *Nursery Suite* because I didn't as yet have one on CD. I also bought slim booklets concerning Elgar's fascination with bicycles and young women, remarking wittily to the man behind the counter that I would have expected the latter to be a much bigger volume.

With 'The Wagon Passes' blasting out from the Morgan's audio, I then essayed a mellifluously named yet circuitous cross country journey, by way of Tinker's Cross and Cobbler's Corner to Berrow Green, where I joined the B4197 and made my way northwards to Martley. In the continued absence of tearooms, I pulled in at the Post Office Stores at that village and went inside for a bottle of pop and a bag of crisps.

"Mum, look at that yellow car!" said a small girl's voice behind me.

"Yes, well you'll have to get a very good job when you grow up to afford a car like that," was the measured parental response.

Out of Martley which, according to the *Shell Guide* is 'a village of several nice houses of the "middling sort"', the B4204 to Tenbury Wells climbs steeply through rocking sandstone cuttings before plunging down into the fecund valley of the Teme, and crossing the river at Ham Bridge. What wonderful countryside. No wonder the music poured out of Elgar after cycle rides in landscapes as inspirational as this. Turning right on to an ascending by-road whose verges were thick with meadowsweet and cranesbill, I gave thought to writing some music myself, perhaps a concerto for orchestra and sports car. Soon the road was wooded, hilly and almost Welsh. I was pushing Worcestershire to its boundaries, reaching Shelsley Walsh at a quarter to four.

How did you know I was coming here? I who know nothing about sports car trials or hill racing. Perhaps the Morgan had made up its mind long ago, and it was me who was being taken for a ride. Not knowing what to expect, but feeling sure that whatever I encountered would be worthwhile, I turned off the road at the foot of a steep escarpment and found myself on a race track of sorts. It climbed steeply ahead through the trees, overlooked by commentary boxes perched on stilts with tannoys sticking prominently from their timbered sides. To the right, on steep slopes cut out of the trees stood a series of benched ampitheatres for the comfort of spectators. There appeared to be no obstacle to me giving it a try. In the absence of a race meeting, informality reigned. Any lunatic could have a go.

Before I set off, however, I want you to get this escapade in context, in as much that I have not attended a race meeting, or a rally, or any other kind of motor event (other than the ritual ten thousand mile servicing of my Toyota) since I went to Mallory Park as a disinterested five year old. So what you are about to witness is the sad attempt of a fifty something to make up for lost time. I would also add, for the nervous of disposition, that there will be scenes of a disturbing nature, should you choose to read on, and that you are perfectly at liberty to put the book quietly away on your shelves without proceeding any further, being, I'm sure, aware that there are no more pages left after this one.

At first I proceeded gingerly, accelerating gently up the steep slope for a few hundred yards until it curved sharply to the left. But egged on by the cries of an imaginary crowd, and encouraged by a growing, if unauthenticated confidence, I let the car have its head, surging forward as the road essayed an uphill S bend through the woods. My favoured driving position prevented me from reading the speedometer because the steering wheel was in the way, but it seemed as though I was hurtling along. After the last bend the road runs straight for the finishing line, a few hundred yards beyond the edge of the woods. The Morgan's temptation to accelerate was too acute to resist and I did nothing to intervene. Suddenly, goodness knows why, but alarmingly, terrifyingly, the car began to hunt from side to side. An experienced driver might have anticipated such erratic behaviour. Perhaps I had come too quickly out of the bend. Instinct told me that braking might be a bad option. In the nano-seconds that all this was taking place, a strange detached calm cut in. I suppose the car must have swerved from side to side half a dozen times before I regained control. I crossed the finish in a straight line and breathed a sigh of gratitude, coming to a halt by a sign which read: 'Motor Racing Can Be Dangerous'.

*   *   *

Come over here and sit down. I have a confession to make. *The Morgan isn't mine!* Charles Morgan very kindly loaned it to me for the eight weeks it took to make the journeys in this book. I am sorry if I've led you up the garden path, but the worst I can stand accused of is being economical with the truth.

So after the thrills and spills of Shelsley Walsh, the reality of a sad drive back to Malvern Link to deposit the car. I got there just after six, filled up with petrol and drove down Pickersleigh Avenue. The office was empty but a guy called Mark Baldwin had been expecting me.

"Had a bit of a dink, have we?" he gestured towards a dent on the mud guard.

"Oh no, that's not me," I replied sheepishly, blithely forgetting that I might have been ringing Morgan to come and get what was left of their car from Shelsley Walsh. "It was like that when I collected it," I added, in self defence.

Mark gave me a lift to the station, though I would have been happy to walk off the pain of parting. At the station I got out quickly and didn't look back, conscious only of a yellow blur roaring away into the distance. It was the end of a holiday romance with the sort of car I wouldn't normally expect to get involved with. A life-enhancing friend I wouldn't necessarily see again. All I knew for certain, was that it would be a terrible anti-climax to drive a 'normal' car again.

I booked a single ticket to Burton-on-Trent and sought consolation at Lady Foley's refreshment room. Coffee cake and a pot of tea, for *one*. I took the tray out on to the platform where elegant cast iron tables and chairs are thoughtfully provided for patrons. Slowly munching the cake I let my mind wander back over the nine journeys which me and 'my' Morgan had made, just as Beethoven might have allowed himself the luxury of considering, in retrospect, the strengths and weaknesses (ridiculous!) of his nine symphonies. Because *my* journeys *had* been like symphonies, with beginnings and middles and ends and moments of great beauty and moments when nothing seemed to be happening at all. Had I a favourite? Can you differentiate among your children? Were there itineraries I would have changed? Of course, just as in life there are alternative directions one might have taken with the benefit of hindsight.

I poured the tea, dark brown, how I like it. A train paused at the opposite platform, Hereford bound, making me wish I was just setting out, all over again. But the Morgan was back with its maker, much as I must go back to mine in due course. And having reached fifty, that day is over the fold in the map and clearly legible, though at what scale the map is drawn to, I cannot decipher.

Time Trials at Shelsley Walsh

WARNING
MOTOR SPORT
CAN BE
DANGEROUS

Index

The Author

Michael Pearson has been occupying progressively more space on the planet for fifty years, though, unlike other dictators, he has no firm plans for further expansion, quite the opposite in fact, once his new fitness regime can be firmly installed.

He first sprang to fame as a compiler of guide books over twenty years ago, but missed his footing, thereafter becoming a shadowy figure venerated solely by a cult following of exceptionally intelligent, perceptive and glamorous people.

He lives with his family in Staffordshire, and on a clear day it is possible to see four power stations from the garden of his 19th Century farm-worker's cottage.

He says of his new book that it closely resembles *Three Men In A Boat* without two of the men and the boat, and with a Morgan in place of Montmorency. Other comparisons with Jerome K. Jerome are inevitable when one considers that both men have visited Jerome K. Jerome's birthplace in Walsall, though regrettably not simultaneously.

Irresistibly attractive to dogs emerging from ponds and independent financial consultants, Michael is currently working behind the scenes with various Government agencies to bring lasting peace, stability, and up to eight new fast food franchises, to The Dukeries.